THE ORGANIZED WRITER

THE ORGANIZED WRITER

A Brief Rhetoric

Edward Proffitt

Manhattan College

Mayfield Publishing Company

Mountain View, California

London • Toronto

Library of Congress Cataloging-in-Publication Data

Proffitt, Edward.
    The organized writer : a brief rhetoric / Edward Proffitt.
       p.   cm.
    Includes index.
    ISBN 1-55934-118-1
    1. English language—Rhetoric.   I. Title.
PE1408.P77   1991
808'.042—dc20   91-36782
                                                                CIP

Manufactured in the United States of America
10 9 8 7 6 5 4 3 2 1

Mayfield Publishing Company
1240 Villa Street
Mountain View, California 94041

Sponsoring editor, Thomas Broadbent; managing editor, Linda Toy; production editors, Sondra Glider and Lynn Rabin Bauer; manuscript editor, Joan Pendleton; text and cover designer, Gary Head. Cover photo: Rod Planck/Tom Stack & Associates. The text was set in 10.5/13 Janson by G & S Typesetters, Inc. and printed on 50# Finch Opaque by Maple-Vail Book Manufacturing Group.

Text Credits: Parts of Appendix II reprinted from *Reading and Writing About Short Fiction* by Edward Proffitt. Reprinted by permission of Harcourt Brace Jovanovich. Pages 181–186, adaptation of "Term paper" from *The Writer's Options*, Third Edition by Donald A. Daiker et al. Copyright © 1986 by Harper & Row, Publishers Inc. Reprinted by permission of HarperCollins Publishers Inc.

To Alberta Mehr
in the bond of friendship

Preface

The Organized Writer aims to provide, as concisely as possible, all that a book can teach a college student about writing expository papers (the term *expository* is used broadly here to encompass most nonfiction prose). The book is brief so that its audience can spend as much time as possible on the activities that are most essential and instructive: writing, and talking about writing, in the classroom.

Chapter 1 deals with the functions and types of expository writing and outlines the writing process. Chapter 2 focuses on the thesis: what it is, how it is formed and stated, how the writer follows through on the thesis statement and its implications, and where the statement can be placed and how the writer can prepare the reader for it. Chapters 3 and 4 tackle organization, with an emphasis on coherence and ways of achieving it through transition. Chapter 5 examines some uses of narration and figurative language, discusses titles, and closes with a distinction between theme and thesis. Chapter 6 considers style, centering on diction and syntax.

The Organized Writer, then, goes into every aspect of the rhetoric of exposition that most writers are likely to need to know. But at the heart of the book—its central concern and binding force—is the subject of organization, which includes transition and coherence. A writing teacher myself, I know (and am reminded with each new class) that organization and coherence are the greatest stumbling blocks that students face in writing papers. And this is as true of most seniors as it is of freshmen. For the same reason, I place special emphasis on revision, or how in the rewriting stage of the writing process one can forge a coherent organization from the mass of ideas in a first draft. Another feature of the book, one I believe unique, is a demonstration in Chapter 4 of how to revise a paper that is basically sound but that, as first presented, tends to lose focus and point (also matters of organization and coherence). Even in the last chapter, on style, the subject of coherence is kept in sight. The section on sentence variety, for instance, shows why a passage consisting of a string of simple sentences is almost sure to be incoherent and how such incoherence can be corrected.

Fully eighty percent of the sample paragraphs and papers in this text are by students, most of whom are named. It's easy enough, of course, for a teacher to write such samples. But a teacher's samples never sound quite right, never have the authenticity that samples should have to be effective. The student samples used in this book, I've found, work well in demonstrating the points at hand.

The exercises at the end of each chapter follow the sequence of topics in the chapter. They are designed not only to reinforce the various points and to allow students to test their grasp of the material but also, simply, to be fun. Most of these exercises have been honed in class, and so I feel confident in saying that they combine instruction and pleasure.

Two appendixes are provided, one a glossary of usage and the other a guide to preparing and documenting research papers.

My guiding belief and principle, reflected in every aspect of *The Organized Writer*, is that students can be brought to write coherently if shown how. And I have found that once a student understands organization and coherence, such relatively minor problems as difficulties with mechanics can be tackled with much greater ease. To think clearly is to think in an organized fashion; and once one starts to think in an organized fashion, writing becomes less formidable and appears as what it really is, a game, a puzzle of pieces to be fitted together, something that is always a challenge yet also can be a delight.

ACKNOWLEDGMENTS

As always, I am indebted to my wife, Nancy, for reading drafts and proof. I am also grateful to Manhattan College for allowing me to teach both regular and advanced composition. My experience in these courses over many years underpins this book. I am especially indebted to Dr. Mary Ann O'Donnell for her expert commentary on drafts as well as for the graciousness of her remarks. Finally, I thank Tom Broadbent, my editor and friend, and all his colleagues at Mayfield Publishing Company who have contributed to making this book.

Contents

Preface   vii

1   Expository Writing: What It Is and How It Is Done   1

THE GOALS OF EXPOSITORY WRITING   1

FUNCTION AND TYPES OF EXPOSITORY WRITING   2

Informational   2

Analytic   3

Persuasive   3

Examples of the Three Types   4

WRITING FOR AN AUDIENCE   7

THE WRITING PROCESS   9

Prewriting   10

Writing: The First Draft   11

Rewriting: The Second Draft and Thereafter   12

Proofing and Titling   13

EXERCISES   14

2   The Thesis   17

TOPIC, OPINION, AND THESIS   17

"My Dog," SANDRA CALVI   18

"The Jaspers"   20

FORMULATING AND STATING A THESIS   21

    Brainstorming   22

    Freewriting   22

    Sleeping on It   23

FOLLOWING THROUGH   24

    "'Useless' versus Useful Knowledge"   26

DECIDING WHERE TO STATE THE THESIS   27

    "Rushing," MAUREEN DEGNAN   28

BEGINNINGS: THE THESIS PARAGRAPH   29

    Analogy   30

    Contrast   30

    Anecdote   31

    Familiar to Unfamiliar   33

    General to Particular   34

REVISION OF A FUNNEL PARAGRAPH   34

EXERCISES   36

3   Organization I: Fundamentals   38

TRANSITION   38

    "The Jaspers" (and Revision)   39

    "Three Months with the Aboto," TRACY MASUCCI   44

UNITY AND COHERENCE   46

BASIC PATTERNS OF ORGANIZATION   52

    Chronology   53

    Spatial Sequence   53

    Comparison and Contrast   54

    Enumeration   56

    Order of Climax   58

EXERCISES 59

4   Organization II: Paragraph to Paper   66

ENDINGS 66

Summarizing and Restating 66

Analogy 67

Question and Answer 68

The Reverse Funnel 68

MIDDLES 70

Sample Paper: "The Problem of Choice" 72

Major and Minor Supports 75

Outlining 76

Paragraphing 78

Paragraph Development 78

Exemplification 80

Definition 81

Appeal to Authority 81

Analogy 82

ARRANGING MIDDLE PARAGRAPHS 82

Chronology 83

"Memories of Me," LAURA LALAINA 83

Spatial Sequence 84

"Self-Expression," CIARAN MCKEEVER 84

Comparison and Contrast 85

"A Matter of Face," TRACY MASUCCI 85

Enumeration 86

"My Summer Job," CLAIRE MCMAHON 86

Order of Climax 87

"The Air, the Water, the Waste," AHN JI-HOON 87

Dialectical Structure   88

    "Dialectical Spirituality," MARYANN MCCARRA   89

REVISING A GOOD PAPER   90

    "Organizational Cultures: A Contrast," LAURA LALAINA   90

EXERCISES   94

    "Types of Men," SANDRA CALVI   95

    "Entertaining a Child," TERENCE MULGREW   99

5   Other Aspects of Expository Writing   100

NARRATION   100

    "So Much for Philosophy!" SANDRA CALVI   100

DIALOGUE AND FICTIONAL DETAIL   103

TONE AND VOICE   104

THE CHARACTER SKETCH   108

    "My Best Friend," JENNIFER CARROLL   108

SYMBOLISM   109

METAPHORICAL LANGUAGE   111

    "The Feud Burns On," TERENCE MULGREW   112

    Some Pitfalls of Metaphor   112

SOUND AND RHYTHM   114

TITLES   116

THEME AND THESIS   117

EXERCISES   117

    "Body and Soul," P. J. LEVINS   119

6   Style   121

DICTION   121

    "Party Buddies," EDWARD HOYT   122

"Court Day," WILLIAM O'CONNELL   123

Two Styles: A Contrast and Prescription   127

SYNTAX   130

Loose Syntax   132

Periodic Syntax   133

Parallel Syntax   134

Balanced Syntax   137

SENTENCE VARIETY   137

Repositioning and Substitution   139

Special Effects   141

Paring Down   141

When Not to Pare   144

CHANGING CONSTRUCTIONS   146

EXERCISES   148

Appendix I: A Short Glossary of Usage   155

Appendix II: A Brief Guide to the Use and Documentation of Sources and Related Matters   168

USING SOURCES   168

Plagiarism   168

Referring to Titles   168

Continuous versus Blocked Quotations   169

Changing Punctuation   170

Ellipsis and Square Brackets   171

Fitting Quotations with Contexts   172

Introducing Quotations   172

Quotation, Summary, and Paraphrase   173

SOURCES: PRIMARY AND SECONDARY   173

CITING SOURCES   174

    Citing Continuous versus Blocked Quotations   175

    Three Problem Spots   175

THE WORKS CITED LIST   176

    Books and Journal Articles   177

    Anthologies   178

    A Work in an Anthology   178

    A Newspaper Article   179

    Two or More Works by the Same Author   180

SAMPLE WORKS CITED LIST AND SAMPLE MANUSCRIPT   180

Index   187

THE ORGANIZED WRITER

Writing: What It Is and How It Is Done

THE GOALS OF EXPOSITORY WRITING

"How can I know what I think till I see what I say?" says a character in an E. M. Forster novel. Exactly so. In large part we write in order to know, especially to know our own minds. To be sure, we write to let others know what we think; and as writers we must never forget the audience we're addressing. Still, the potential of writing to show us ourselves is what's most exciting about it.

But that is exactly why writing is also difficult. It's hard to articulate in an orderly fashion ideas and feelings that whirl around in one's head and get all jumbled up, to iron them out and put them into sentences and paragraphs that are logical and comprehensible in their patterns. It's hard for everybody. I sometimes think that the difference between experienced and inexperienced writers is that experienced writers know how difficult writing is. It is difficult because it requires not only that we articulate our thoughts and feelings but, again, that we do so in an organized manner. Without organization, comprehension is impossible; without organization, your writing will communicate neither to your reader nor, in any genuinely significant way, to you yourself.

Here is where rhetoric comes in. The Greeks and Romans defined rhetoric as the art of persuasion. But to persuade, you must communicate, and to communicate you must impose an order on your material so that it can be understood. At heart, then, rhetoric is the art of organization.

Though rhetoric entails other considerations as well—style, for instance—and though we shall consider these other aspects of rhetoric in due course, our emphasis will be on coherent organization, coherence being the base of good writing. Above all else, the writer must learn to

1

relate thoughts so that they form a coherent whole. If you learn nothing else from this book but how to organize material and, thus, how to write coherently, you will have learned enough to be, if not a great writer, a writer who can articulate thoughts and feelings for whatever purpose is at hand.

Organizing, relating, making matters clear, both for oneself and others—those, I believe, are the basic goals of any kind of writing, but especially of the kind this book will focus on. Broadly called expository prose, it is the kind of writing you're reading right now and the kind most people, especially college students, write most often: diaries and journals, reports, term papers, and so forth.

FUNCTION AND TYPES OF EXPOSITORY WRITING

Expository prose is prose designed to "expose" and examine some aspect of a topic: that is, to set forth facts, ideas and feelings, and informed judgments in an orderly fashion. Its purpose is to come to a fuller understanding of some aspect of a topic and to communicate that understanding to the intended audience. *In an orderly fashion* is the key phrase. Because exposition has ready understanding as its primary goal, its greatest asset is clarity; and clarity demands that facts, ideas and feelings, and informed judgments be set forth point by point, with each point clearly related to the next and with some overall plan of movement clearly followed.

In this book we will be concerned with three main types of expository prose: informational, analytic, and persuasive.

Informational

As the name suggests, informational prose presents (or exposes) information. Should you do research on Gandhi or Eleanor Roosevelt or St. Paul, for instance, and write up what you find, your write-up would be informational. Informational prose places two demands on the writer: first, it must be factual; second, like all expository prose, it must proceed in an orderly fashion. It requires that the writer choose some mode of organization according to the nature of the material and follow through on that choice.

Analytic

From the Greek meaning "to break up," analysis entails first the breaking of a subject into its component parts and then a detailed examination part by part. Take a typical college paper. You are asked to write a paper analyzing, say, why the Nazis were able to gain power in the 1930s. No doubt there are a number of reasons: the disastrous inflation of the 1920s, the consequent unemployment and misery, the chaotic conditions resulting from communist riots, the German character as conditioned by Bismarck and by the domination of Prussia in the nineteenth century, and so forth. Having broken the subject into some of its parts, you would proceed by discussing each in a paragraph or perhaps a cluster of paragraphs. You must also make sure to relate each of these segments to the segments coming before and after, and to arrange the segments according to some overall plan (for instance, building to the most important item last). All of this is what analysis entails.

Analytic prose incorporates a good deal of information. Certainly, the hypothetical paper on the rise of Nazism would encompass as many facts as any purely informational paper. But analytic prose is different in purpose from straight informational prose. The purpose of analytic prose is not merely to set forth facts but also, by way of facts, to uncover and clarify meaning. In other words, when writing an analysis, one brings factual material to bear for the purpose of discovering and then backing up an interpretation. For this reason, analytic prose is more complex than informational. Informational prose—for instance, the précis, the plot summary, the biographical sketch—is generally what high-school students are called upon to write. College students are most often asked to write analytic prose, for the primary goal of college is to impart the ability to analyze.

Persuasive

Analytic prose necessarily overlaps with persuasive: when writing an analysis, you wish the reader to accept your ideas; and when trying to persuade a reader, you must analyze the reasons for the position you wish the reader to accept. And both analytic and persuasive prose incorporate information. But the writer of persuasive prose does not, finally, seek to clarify ideas so much as to sway the reader to accept and adopt the writer's position.

For instance, should you write a paper arguing the merits of capital punishment or the reasons why you are against it, you would be engaged in writing persuasive prose, for your primary object would be to sway your reader to your point of view. Reviews—of books, movies, television shows—are usually of the same order. Aimed at convincing the reader of a work's merit (or lack of merit), a typical review proceeds to analyze that work to establish why it is or isn't (according to the reviewer) worth reading or seeing. To be sure, analysis comes into play, but the goal is persuasion.

Examples of the Three Types

The difference between the three types of exposition, indeed, can be summed up in terms of goal: setting forth of factual material (informational); clarifying and arguing ideas with factual material (analytic); defending judgments aroused by ideas (persuasive). The paragraphs that follow exemplify each type of prose in turn. All three concern Frost's "The Road Not Taken."

The Road Not Taken

ROBERT FROST

Two roads diverged in a yellow wood,
And sorry I could not travel both
And be one traveler, long I stood
And looked down one as far as I could
To where it bent in the undergrowth;   5

Then took the other, as just as fair,
And having perhaps the better claim,
Because it was grassy and wanted wear;
Though as for that the passing there
Had worn them really about the same,   10

And both that morning equally lay
In leaves no step had trodden black.
Oh, I kept the first for another day!

Yet knowing how way leads on to way,
I doubted if I should ever come back.   15

I shall be telling this with a sigh
Somewhere ages and ages hence:
Two roads diverged in a wood, and I—
I took the one less traveled by,
And that has made all the difference.   20

Informational

The speaker of Robert Frost's "The Road Not Taken" tells of how he came to a fork in the road and, therefore, of his having to make a choice as to which path to follow. He would like to have traveled both, he says, but, since he could not, he chose the road that "was grassy and wanted wear." Or was it really different after all? After suggesting that the two roads were "about the same," Frost's speaker says that he might come back and travel the other road on another day, although, given how things fall out, he probably won't. In the last stanza, he projects himself into the future and says that sometime "ages and ages hence" he will tell the story of the two roads and say that he "took the one less traveled by."

This paragraph amounts to a factual description of what is said in the poem. No interpretation is offered nor any judgment of its merit made.

Analytic

Given that traveling on a road generally symbolizes life's journey and, thus, that a fork in the road symbolizes a choice as to which way one's life is to go, Robert Frost's "The Road Not Taken" dramatizes the difficulty we most often have when it comes to making an important choice. One source of that difficulty is expressed at the beginning of the poem through its speaker's stated regret at having had to make a choice at all ("sorry I could not travel both"): we wish to eat our cake and have it too. But we must make choices. So we look for a basis upon which to choose. The basis Frost's speaker points to for his choice is that the road he chose sometime back "was grassy and wanted wear." Yet immediately he goes on to tell us that actually the two roads were about equally "worn" and equally covered in leaves "no step had trodden black." Thus the choice was doubly difficult because there was no clear basis upon which to make it. No doubt, this is a prime reason for the speaker's ambivalence, expressed by the poem's title and by his desire to keep the other road "for another day." In the last stanza of the poem, the speaker moves from the past into the distant future and suggests that then he will say that his reason for choosing the road he did was that it was "the one less traveled by." But we know that this will be merely a rationalization for a choice made reluctantly and without any real basis. The emotional ambiguity of the last stanza also suggests the reluctance of the speaker as well as his uneasiness with the choice made: Will the "sigh" be one of satisfaction or of regret? Will the "difference" be for the better or the worse? We never know beforehand what the outcome of a choice will be, just as more often than not we have no real basis for making it in the first place. "The Road Not Taken," then, concerns our difficulty generally with making important choices: our reluctance to choose; our mixed feelings once we have chosen; and our tendency to rationalize our choices at some later date. We must make choices, of course; but choosing is difficult for us, both because of the unknowns of the outer world and especially because of the conflicts within.

In this paragraph, an interpretation is offered and then demonstrated. The material is broken into three parts (summarized in the next to last sentence) and taken up part by part. The discussion serves to clarify and validate the interpretation stated in the first sentence.

Persuasive

Robert Frost's "The Road Not Taken" may seem ambiguous to some, who, failing to distinguish between the poem and its speaker, therefore pronounce Frost's poem a failure. Though, of course, a poem may be great despite its ambiguity—or even because of it— Frost's poem is in no way ambiguous. It is the emotional state of its speaker that is ambiguous, not the poem itself. Indeed, "The Road Not Taken" is effective because it lucidly captures the wavering and uncertain feelings of its wayfaring speaker, who is unable to make up his mind about the choice he made as to roads. Was it the right one? He cannot say. So he regrets having had to choose at all, his regret being suggested by the poem's title (why not "The Road Taken"?) and the overt statements of lines 2 ("sorry I could not travel both") and 13 ("I kept the first for another day"). His feelings, then, are mixed, complex, ambiguous. And was his choice well founded? He wants it to be so. Thus, he says that he chose the road he did "Because it was grassy and wanted wear." But in all candor, he has to contradict himself with the truth that the roads were "really about the same" (lines 9–12). His feelings are ambiguous, then, because the choice itself was ambiguous. Ambiguity of feeling is further suggested in the last stanza with the words "sigh" and "difference." For we're not told what kind of sigh (whether of contentment or despair) or what kind of difference (whether for better or worse). But the poem's crowning ambiguity, or so it seems, is the line "I took the one less traveled by." In fact, however, the line is not at all ambiguous if we realize what the speaker has said: that he will say this "ages and ages hence." That is, he will forget the facts, with all their ambiguity, and iron out the knotty truth with a simple rationalization. In sum, Frost's poem, though itself lucid, concerns ambiguity, the ambiguities of choice and our feelings about making choices. It is a powerful poem because it captures in its short span much that is true about the generally mixed nature of human thoughts and feelings.

Here, though the paragraph entails analysis of one aspect of the poem, the focus is on evaluation. That is, the point of the paragraph is not, finally, to come to a better understanding of the poem but to demonstrate that it is a powerful poem and to suggest why this judgment is valid. Its governing idea, stated in the fourth sentence, is quite different in character, then, from the governing idea stated in the first sentence of the analytic paragraph.

WRITING FOR AN AUDIENCE

Another consideration that we should take up now, at the outset of our study, is the matter of audience. In part, as we've noted, writing is a way of getting to know one's own mind: by being forced to articulate clearly, we can come to know what we really think and feel. I never write without learning something about myself, and most other writers, I believe, would concur. Writing is also a way of learning about virtually any subject. I once had a professor who said that whenever he found that he didn't know something he wanted to know, he would write a book about it.

Learning—whether about the self or the rest of creation—is a private motive for writing. Journals, diaries, and the like are also usually private, written only for oneself. But here we start to approach the question of audience, even if the audience is only oneself. For many years I have kept a journal of important events in my life, recording a paragraph or two for each event. Usually, my paragraphs prove coherent and I know, even years later, what I meant. But sometimes they are baffling; I simply cannot make out what on earth I meant. When I wrote those particular entries, I simply didn't consider my audience—me. And when coming back to something he or she wrote years before, a writer really is like an audience—that is, someone else. We change, so our past selves can seem as distinct from us in the present as other people are distinct.

In any event, we usually write for other people as well as ourselves, and this is especially true of exposition. In writing a term paper, for instance, you should learn something about your subject as well as something about your thoughts and feelings with regard to that subject; but with a term paper, you clearly have an audience, and you must keep that fact uppermost in mind. In writing a report, a term paper, an essay of any kind, your purpose is mainly to communicate. Therefore, you must consider the audience you mean to communicate with. When a writer fails to consider the intended audience, communication is sure to be hampered.

But you shouldn't consider judging an audience and writing with that audience in mind to be a burden. In fact, keeping your audience in mind can help you solve many problems that come up during the writing process. Suppose, for example, that you were a research physicist and had to write a speech on quarks for an audience of high-school students. You would realize, surely, that you would have to simplify your presentation and define all terms. If you didn't, you would probably put your audience to sleep or be booed off stage. On the other hand, if you were giving a speech on the same subject to a group of experts in the field, you could rely on their knowing your terms and being able to deal with the subject in its complexity. For this audience you would not want to define most terms, lest you should be thought condescending, and you would want to treat your subject in greater depth. In each case, your audience would be your measuring rod. In each case, your decisions about diction (word choice), syntax (the ways of putting words together), depth of treatment, and so forth would be made easier by considering your intended audience. By measuring everything against the audience intended, you will find that many of the problems that the writing process inevitably entails all but solve themselves.

But how is your audience to be identified? I always tell my own students to write with the class in mind: for me in part, since I am a member of the class, but mainly for their fellow students. After all, they, or people like them, will constitute each student's audience in the future. As to the present, writing with your own classmates in mind will give you experience in writing for an audience. What do they know? What don't they know? If you're writing on something that has been taken up in class—a short story, say, or an historical event—your audience can be assumed to be familiar with your topic if not with your particular approach to it or the specific arguments you will use to elucidate your point. You need not, therefore, waste precious space summarizing a plot or describing the event in question. Nor need you define any terms that you know your audience is acquainted with because they have been discussed in class. By defining your audience and keeping it in view, you will find that the problem of deciding what to include and what to leave out is greatly simplified, as are decisions about vocabulary and style in general. In writing this book, for instance, I have a typical college audience in mind. Knowing my audience (I've taught for twenty-five years), I know just how far I should go with regard to the difficulty of my vocabulary, the complexity of my syntax, and so forth. If I were writing for sixth-graders or for professors, my decisions would be different in each case. Assessing and remembering my audience help guide me through the hundreds of decisions that writing entails. If you guide yourself similarly, you will find the process of writing to be much less difficult than it probably has been if you haven't been taking your audience into account.

THE WRITING PROCESS

Writing that communicates requires planning and thought. Though, to be sure, an essay should have about it a sense of verve, and the best expository prose may seem inspired, the writing of any kind of exposition demands deliberation and organization. It demands as well an organized approach. Whatever one writes in whatever kind of format, it is essential to divide the work into stages and to proceed step by step. It is for this reason that expository writing is spoken of as a process. Broadly, the process has four stages—prewriting, writing, rewriting, and proofing—and each entails a series of distinct steps. Here we'll just sketch the stages and the steps that each stage comprises. Subsequent chapters will fill in the details.

Prewriting

Prewriting covers everything you do before you actually sit down to write. For instance, say that you are assigned to write a paper on a short story. The first thing you would have to do, obviously, is to read the story. Since you would know that you are going to write a paper on it, you would do well to take notes as you read, jotting down any ideas the story stimulates in you and any questions you have about it, noting any feelings it evokes, and perhaps recording what you think the story means in general terms. The next logical step would be to mull over your notes and, ideally, to read the story again, now testing your ideas, seeking answers to your questions, and firming up your sense of what the story means. Then you would have to develop an idea, something to write about—a thesis (see Chapter 2). In doing so, you should look to yourself and decide what really interests you. Good writing demands personal commitment. Of course, your choice must also be geared to the number of pages you intend to write. Some ideas might be too broad and some too narrow in this regard. Next, with an interesting idea that seems appropriate to the scope of your projected paper, you'd look over your notes to find or devise a general plan of organization. Now you would be ready to begin writing.

These steps in the prewriting phase are more or less the same for any topic. In writing a paper on Rembrandt's *The Nightwatch*, for example, you would have to look at the painting (the equivalent of reading a story) and look at it again, developing an idea to write about and some plan of organization from the notes you would take while studying the painting. (Notes are best taken on separate slips of paper or index cards, one note per slip or card. You'll see why shortly.) Again, you should look to yourself to find an idea that really stimulates you and that you want to write about. Or say that you have to write a paper on the Battle of Waterloo and are given a choice of topics: why the British won, the effect of Napoleon's defeat on the French economy, the effect on the British psyche, and so forth. It is to be hoped that one or another of the given topics interests you. Once more, your interest should guide your choice. Here, of course, you would have to research your subject, research being a possible step in the prewriting phase. Again you would take notes, and again you would have to develop a specific idea to write about and some plan of organization. As you can see, no matter what the subject, the steps of the prewriting phase are similar in pattern, if not in every detail.

Writing: The First Draft

The writing phase, or what one does during it, is also basically the same whatever the specific subject might be. Here I shall use my own writing habits as an example. Although writers go about writing in various ways, my way is probably typical. After I have finished all the preparations I'm going to do, thought out all I can think out beforehand, finished, in other words, the prewriting stage, I wind up with a stack of notes, one note per slip of paper. Sitting down at my desk, I look through these notes carefully, dividing them into categories and setting aside anything that might be of use for the beginning and for the end. (None of this is possible, obviously, if notes are not taken separately in the first place, one note per slip—thus, the importance of doing so.) Categorizing my notes leads to a general sense of organization, enough of a sense to get me going. With some thought of a possible organization in mind, then, I begin to write.

Usually, I have a firm idea—or thesis—in mind. So, usually, I begin at the beginning, with a paragraph or more leading to and stating my main idea. All writers don't begin this way, however, and I myself have occasionally started in the middle; once, I actually wrote the ending first. Where you begin is of no consequence. At this stage of the writing process, what matters is just getting something down on paper (or, if you work on a computer, up on the screen). Still, to be candid, I do like to begin at the beginning, with a statement of what it is I plan to discuss. That helps to keep me on track. And if things take an unexpected turn—as often happens—the beginning can always be rewritten later. Organization, too, can be modified or altered entirely at a later stage. But as I begin to write, I usually have a sense of where I am going. My notes, which ease me into writing by giving me something to write about (I would be lost without them), also help me to organize my thoughts (remember, the notes are categorized by this point) and to stay on target more or less. But I don't restrain myself too much as I write a first draft (especially now that I am writing on a computer, which makes changes easy). I let the juices flow as much as possible, the creativity of the unconscious direct me as it will. I usually wind up with a first draft that I feel is a good start.

Before we move on, I want to put in a plug for the unconscious, which I've barely mentioned but which most writers know to be their greatest ally. Days and even weeks before I am going to begin a writing project, I start to think about it on and off. Even when I'm not consciously thinking about it, it's there, somewhere in the back of my mind. I let it come to consciousness especially when I have nothing better to occupy my thoughts— when I'm driving to work, for instance, or in the shower. And frequently— especially when I'm falling asleep—ideas force themselves forward of their own accord. By the time I'm ready to write, I usually have a good deal to write about. The only disadvantage of this kind of deliberate tapping of the unconscious is that I must keep a pad and pen available at all times. I never know when the unconscious will speak.

Rewriting: The Second Draft and Thereafter

After the initial writing phase, I become a critic. My first draft behind me, I look with a critic's eye at what I've written. Once my initial despair passes, I get down to the basic work of writing, which is rewriting. Many writers, myself included, consider this phase of the writing process the most important. But like the other phases, rewriting must proceed in steps, for the brain cannot do everything at once. The mapping out of a workable series of steps greatly eases the difficulty of writing.

Here are the steps in the rewriting phase that I follow, and I suggest that you do the same. Putting out of your mind what you intended to say and looking carefully at what you actually have said, first check what you have written, paragraph by paragraph, against your thesis statement. Should you find that you've wandered away from the point, either bring the suspect passage into line or cut it out. You may even find that most of your paper doesn't go with your controlling idea. In such a case, one solution would be to restate your idea so that it does fit. Because writing is a process, you never truly know what you have to say until you've said it. It's not surprising, therefore, that writers sometimes discover along the way that they actually have something other to say than what they initially thought they were going to say. Second, check the arrangement of your paragraphs to make sure that they follow logically and move easily from

one to the next. You might find that some paragraphs need to be reposi-
tioned. So reposition, making sure to relate paragraphs as now positioned
as well as all material within each paragraph. (Exactly how, we'll take up
later in the book.) Finally, every time you look over what you've written,
keep an eye out for what can be polished—a better word here, a more
concise way of putting something there—and polish as you go.

From what I've said, you might get the idea that the primary business
of rewriting is to make sure that everything is to the point and follows as
logically and gracefully as possible. If so, you are exactly right. In writing
a first draft, your focus should be on what you have to say. In writing a
second draft, it should be on how you say it, especially on how the segments of your paper go together—that is, on organization. Remember,
comprehensible organization is the key to communication. The most
beautiful sentences in the world, if just jumbled together, would communicate many separate ideas, perhaps, but nothing in particular. In
short, the rewriting phase is the most important because it is in this phase
that you beat your material into shape.

Proofing and Titling

When you have a final draft in hand, what's left is careful proofreading. Because, again, the brain cannot do everything at once, proofreading
should also be done in steps. As I always suggest to my own students (and
such is my own practice, too), read your final draft once through, checking for subject-verb agreement errors only. Then read it again, checking
only for pronoun reference and agreement. All three are potential problem spots and therefore require special attention. Next, read your paper
for spelling, punctuation, and other matters of mechanics, preferably
aloud so that you can also check the sound of your prose. Watch especially for errors that you know that you are prone to make. As to sound,
if your writing does not sound like you, something is wrong. Go back and
rephrase anything that seems stilted or roundabout.

After you have finished with these steps, give your paper a title. To
be sure, you may have a tentative title in mind even before you start
writing. But it is best to wait until the last to make a final decision about
a title. You can't be sure of what you're going to say until you've said it,
so a title can never be more than tentative until the end. But be sure to
give everything you write (unless it's a letter or a grocery list, of course)
a title. Remember that a title—the first thing a reader sees—focuses the

reader's attention and draws the reader in. Titles are functional, then, and should be chosen with care. (Later, we'll look at what makes a good title and how one should go about choosing one.)

Having decided on a title, you're now ready for the final draft—that is, the final typing or printout. Once this is in hand, all that remains is a final check for typographical errors. Then it's on to the next assignment. If you follow the steps outlined here and keep following them assignment after assignment, they will become habitual. Then, assuredly, you will find that, since your writing process is itself coherent, you now think coherently and so write with greater ease than you ever did before.

In this introductory chapter we have looked at expository prose in general: its goals, both private and public; its function and types—informational, analytic, and persuasive; and the importance of a sense of one's audience. We have also examined, in a general way, the writing process itself, its stages—prewriting, writing, rewriting, and proofing—and the steps that each stage entails. Now we shall look at specific aspects of that process. Before we move on, however, here are a few exercises designed to reinforce your understanding of the concepts presented in this chapter. Each subsequent chapter will end with similar exercises, which should help you master the material and make it your own.

EXERCISES

1. Get a topic of a personal nature—for instance, your feelings about your girl-friend or boyfriend, your school, your parents—and write a journal entry stating your feelings in such a way that what you write is clear to you. Having done this, write a paragraph on the same material that, hypothetically, you mean to be read not only by you but by other people as well. Have a specific audience in mind as you go about the second task—your brothers and sisters, perhaps, or your classmates, or your parents. Now observe the differences between the journal entry and the paragraph, or between private writing and public. You could go further and write a final paragraph (or more) codifying those differences. Write this paragraph with your classmates and instructor in mind.

2. **a.** Pick one of the following topics, or choose one of your own, and write a purely informational paragraph on it. Your object will be only to describe or recount accurately.

The campus of my school

The last movie I saw

The cold war

A rock group or star

A song sung by that group or star

Vietnam

b. Having completed your informational paragraph, get an idea, a thesis, something about the same topic that you believe and want to argue. For instance,

How the last movie I saw was constructed

Why the cold war is over

What a given song means

Why we were in Vietnam

Now you will have a specific point to make. This paragraph will be analytic.

c. Finally, using the same material, get an idea that entails evaluation and write a persuasive paragraph. For instance,

The campus of my school should be overhauled.

The last movie I saw was great/awful.

Why one rock group—as opposed to others—is my favorite.

We should/should not have been in Vietnam.

Remember that now you will be trying to persuade an audience that the judgment you've made is the correct one. To do so, you must spell out the reasons that led you to that judgment.

3. **a.** Choose something you know about, choose a point to make about it, and then write two analytic paragraphs, one aimed at an audience who knows nothing about your subject area and one aimed at an audience who knows as much as you do about it.

b. If you are female, pretend that you are about to address an all-male audience on a subject that concerns women. Write an outline for this speech and note point by point how you will gear what you say to your male auditors. If you are male, do the same in reverse.

c. Pretend that you are writing a letter to a friend, one paragraph of which concerns your dislike for a particular teacher. Write that paragraph. Now write a paragraph that you mean to send to the dean of your school about the teacher in question. Note the differences between the two paragraphs, differences that spring from the two different audiences.

4.   Take any topic you like and write an analytic or persuasive paragraph or essay deliberately following the steps of the writing process as outlined in this chapter. Be sure to state your point toward the beginning and to check everything you go on to say against that point.

The Thesis

Every piece of writing—report, essay, research paper, and so forth—has a point to make. However, the three types of writing we are concerned with in this book—informational, analytic, and persuasive—differ with regard to the kind of point each entails. The point of an informational report is the information itself or its delivery in an organized way. Writing a brief history of Polish labor unions, for instance, you would state at the beginning of the report what you intend to do, and then you would do it, organizing your material chronologically, perhaps. There is no room for speculation in a piece of writing like this; everything must be factual. This is where informational prose differs from analytic and persuasive prose. Though analytic and persuasive prose alike incorporate facts, each begins with speculation. That is, the point of both is to argue and support some idea most often stated up front. But whereas the controlling idea of an analytic essay is interpretative—an assessment of meaning—that of a persuasive essay is evaluative—an assessment of worth.

TOPIC, OPINION, AND THESIS

Let's pause over the word *thesis*, which is what the main idea of a piece of analytic or persuasive prose is called. You might be wondering, "What exactly is a thesis? Is it the same thing as the topic of a paper? Or is it just an opinion?" A thesis is neither a topic nor merely an opinion, and the distinctions are important. A topic is simply some aspect of a more general subject area that the writer has chosen to focus on. The thesis is what the writer wishes to say about the topic.

Thinking of Robert Frost's "The Road Not Taken" as a subject area, consider the following possible topics:

The Speaker of Frost's "The Road Not Taken"

Why Not "The Road Taken"?

The Problem of Choice in "The Road Not Taken"

Time Present and Time Future in "The Road Not Taken"

I've deliberately cast these phrases as titles because each could be a title. In fact, titles often indicate topics, stimulating in the reader the question, "What about it?" Having a topic in mind, the writer needs to ask the same question: "The Problem of Choice"—what about it? One answer might be: "In 'The Road Not Taken,' Robert Frost dramatizes the difficulty we most often have when it comes to making important choices." (Note that this possible thesis, interpretative in nature and therefore fit for an analytic essay, is stated in a complete sentence. We shall return to this matter when we get to thesis formulation.)

So a thesis is not a topic. Nor is it a mere opinion. "Oranges are the best fruit there is" is not a thesis but a mere opinion, as impossible to support as it is uninteresting. In contrast, "Oranges may provide a cure for cancer" is a thesis, for conceivably it could be supported by facts and by an appeal to authority (that is, by statements of experts in the field of cancer research). But if you wish to think of a thesis as an opinion, think of it as a kind of opinion *that can be supported by facts and informed judgments*.

And supporting a thesis by facts and informed judgments is the purpose of both analytic and persuasive writing. The thesis provides the controlling idea, which everything else in a paper demonstrates and clarifies. Everything in a paper, then, must relate to its thesis, for a paper is about its thesis and nothing else. Observe how the italicized thesis in the following sample paper (written by a student, like most of the sample papers in this book) controls the development of the paper and how everything said in the paper relates to its thesis.

My Dog

A dog is a man's best friend, as they say, and a woman's, too. Yes, a canine can be a true companion whatever one's sex— playful, loyal, and selfless, never asking anything in return for its friendship. My dog, Smokey, is all of this and more. Sometimes he cheers me up more than any person can, even my boyfriend.

In fact, *when I compare my dog to my boyfriend, I often think that a dog is a better companion than a man.*

In the first place, a dog can't talk. Consequently, it can't scream or ask questions. My boyfriend, on the other hand, often sounds like he's hosting a game of twenty-one questions: "Where were you? Why are you late? Who were you talking with?" It's enough to drive anyone crazy. Moreover, his little game usually results in a screaming match between the two of us. In contrast, should I get home late, Smokey just sits and wags his tail, just as he does when I'm on time. And when I talk to him, he listens—unlike my boyfriend—and never gives me a headache—again, unlike my boyfriend.

In the second place, Smokey doesn't watch television. So I never find him in a comatose state watching a Yankees or a Rams game. When I come home, Smokey always greets me as though I were the most important person on earth. His excitement is infectious. My boyfriend, on the other hand, thinks it is a criminal offense to leave the television set during any sports event. More often than not, he greets me with a grunt when I go to his house and makes a beeline back to the TV. For companionship, I'll take a dog anytime.

In the third place, Smokey asks for nothing more than People Snacks—little dog treats in the shape of doctors, mailmen, and so forth—on occasion. Boyfriends, in contrast, need to be catered to twenty-four hours a day. Sometimes I think that my boyfriend is just a grown child looking for a mother. There he sits in front of the TV and bids me get a snack—oh, nothing like People Snacks; no, he will settle for nothing less than a homemade pizza or two or three Reuben sandwiches. So, while he watches a game, I'm in the kitchen fixing a feast for his highness.

What I don't understand is, if a dog is a man's best friend, how come man and dog are nothing alike? I can't puzzle that one out. But I know one thing for sure: the next time my boyfriend wants a snack, he's going to get People Snacks. If they're good enough for Smokey, they're sure as hell good enough for him!

SANDRA CALVI

The thesis of this essay is that "a dog is a better companion than a man." That thesis is argued (with tongue in cheek in part) point by point.

Each paragraph after the first adheres to the thesis and backs it up, giving reasons why the writer feels as she does. Nothing that does not bear on the thesis and support it, notice, is allowed in. Thus, the paper is coherent as it moves with a sense of inevitability to its conclusion. Contrast this paper now with the following, which has no clear thesis and so no sense of direction.

The Jaspers

First of all you might be wondering, "What is a Jasper?" We get our name from a man named Jasper, who was the head of athletics at Manhattan College a number of years ago. What is a Jasper today? A Jasper is anyone who contributes to the college community. A Jasper is anyone who goes to Manhattan College.

Many students are avid athletes whether they are in league or intramural sports. The cross-country and track teams do extremely well each year. The Lady J's basketball team is also a very impressive team. Swimming is a team that holds its own each year. The men's basketball team has a long way to go, baby. Club basketball does well. Club sports such as golf, tennis, football, volleyball, and hockey can be fun. The gym is open for those who would like to run, take an aerobics class, swim, or organize their own games.

There are many other extracurricular activities, such as Social Action, Amnesty International, Young Republicans, Young Democrats, Peace Club, Student Government, Folk Singers' Club. And it is always possible for anyone to start a club.

Honor societies reward excellent students. There are general excellence and individual honor societies. The activities of honor societies range from printing a journal to sponsoring a speaker. The school sponsors many mixers, movies, and cultural events. There are two semiformal dances held each year, the Jasper Jingle and the Spring Fling. Senior week is a special time for seniors. It is filled with a variety of activities, from the honors convention to the prom.

Of course, who could be a Jasper without going to the bars below campus on Broadway now and again? All of this and so much more make a Jasper.

The main problem with this paper is that, as it stands, it makes no point at all. It may say many things, but it says nothing in particular. It therefore reads like a series of disjointed lists. And that, indeed, is exactly what it is. At every turn the reader wonders, "So? What's your point? What are you trying to tell me?" Though a thesis statement like that at the end of the first paragraph of "My Dog" would not cure all of the ills of "The Jaspers," it would at least give the reader some sense of bearings and the paper some sense of direction and point. But as it stands, without a thesis even implied—much less stated—the paper really is not worth a reader's effort (except as an example of what not to do). By comparing these two student papers, you can see just how important a clear thesis statement is both to the reader and the writer: it is necessary so that your reader will know what you are talking about and so you will too.

FORMULATING AND STATING A THESIS

Formulating a workable thesis is the ultimate task of the prewriting stage of the writing process. But how do you arrive at such a thesis? Well, first you must have a subject area, and from that you draw a topic. For college students, the subject area is usually dictated by the course the student is writing for: fine arts, economics, history, or whatever. Within the appropriate subject area you should always (if given the freedom to do so) choose a topic in light of your own interests. As you saw in Chapter 1, a good rule is first look to yourself. What most stimulates you? What most moves you to want to speak your mind? What might you want to learn more about? For example, Monet's last paintings, all of water lilies, would be a good topic for someone who loves those paintings, perhaps knows something about them, and wants to learn more. Or the rise of Nazi Germany would be a possible topic for someone interested in the history of our century and enthusiastic about researching the subject matter.

Now you need to get a thesis *about* your topic. What do you have to say? What insight do you have to share? What judgment can you support? What about your topic do you want to discuss? But what if no ideas come? Your mind is as blank as the sheet of paper in front of you. First of all, don't just sit there. Get up, do something else, take your mind off your paper entirely. Often when what we seek doesn't come, it later comes unbidden. If still nothing comes to mind, then you might try the following techniques, one or another of which might work for you.

Brainstorming

Get together with a couple of people who are writing on the same topic and brainstorm. Begin with each of you throwing out whatever ideas and feelings you have about the topic and then questioning each other, probing what each has said as you work toward full articulation. For example, say your topic is Robert Frost's "The Road Not Taken." You've read the poem several times but just aren't sure what to say, what would make a strong thesis for the paper you have to write. So you get together with a couple of classmates and talk. Here's an abbreviated scenario:

JOHN: I think the poem is about taking chances, not following the beaten track.

BETH: But why does Frost say the two roads were exactly the same?

YOU: Yeah. I wasn't sure about the end, either. He doesn't say that he took the road less traveled exactly but that he will say it sometime in the future. That's strange.

BETH: Maybe he's saying that he will have forgotten that the roads were actually the same.

JOHN: Yeah. We do that. The brain does that. We remember how we wanted things to be instead of how they were. Maybe that's what the poem is about.

YOU: That gives me an idea!

Now you're off and running. Brainstorming is a good technique for the generation of ideas if other people are available. If you cannot find other people, however, you might try freewriting.

Freewriting

Freewriting is writing without thought. Sit down and, paying no attention to spelling, grammar, or even coherence, write. Just write. Focusing on your topic, write down anything and everything that comes into your mind and keep writing. Don't take the pen from the paper. Keep writing for ten minutes or so. Then read over what you've written, looking for some nugget idea that can be turned into a thesis. I often freewrite myself just to limber up. I recommend the technique for that purpose as well.

Sleeping on It

Freewriting, in part, can tap the unconscious and bring it into play. There is an even more direct way of attempting this. As you go to sleep, think about the topic of the paper you have to do. Mull over your thoughts and feelings as you drift off into unconsciousness. You might just wake up in the morning with an idea for a thesis if not its full articulation. You might even wake up during the middle of the night with an idea you want to write down. Be sure to keep a pencil and pad near just in case.

Though not essential, it is usually advisable to have a fairly clear thesis before starting to write. After all, the more clearly you can know what you are writing about, the easier your job will be. So you should usually formulate at least a tentative thesis at the outset. As you formulate a thesis, remember to take into account the scope of the paper you intend to write. Surely, the thesis of a two-page report must be more limited than that of a thirty-page term paper. In other words, just as your idea cannot be so narrow as to leave you nothing to write, it must not be so broad as to require that you write a book (unless you are writing a book). "The fork in the road in Frost's 'The Road Not Taken' symbolizes a choice on life's journey" is too narrow even for a two-page paper, especially since most people would grant that premise without argument. On the other hand, "The modern dilemma informs Frost's 'The Road Not Taken' " is too broad and unfocused to be of any use to you or your reader.

With regard to scope, a thesis suited to a typical college paper would have to fall somewhere between the two statements just discussed—be broader than the first and narrower than the second. Here, in contrast, are three viable thesis statements, each stated in a complete sentence. *Note:* A thesis cannot be stated in less than one complete sentence, and sometimes a statement requires more than one sentence. So if you don't have at least one complete sentence—that is, a complete statement of an idea—then you may have a topic but you don't have a thesis.

1. In "The Road Not Taken," Frost expresses the dilemma we often face when it comes to making important choices.

2. In their muted colors, gentle brush strokes, and calm surfaces, Monet's last paintings capture the quiet, almost mystical serenity possible to old age.

3. Nazism took hold in Germany in the 1930s for three reasons: the Versailles Treaty of 1919, the inability of the Weimar Republic to govern, and the economic conditions during the 1920s and early 1930s both within and outside of Germany.

Whether you formulate your thesis statement early or late in the writing process, a statement like one of the three preceding must finally be incorporated somewhere in your paper, usually in the beginning. The thesis statement is your statement of purpose, without which your readers can only ask, "So. What's the point?"

In sum, in deciding what to write, let your feelings guide you to a topic. Then decide what it is about the topic you have to say. Write down your answer in at least one complete sentence. Then judge what you have written: Is your statement too broad or too narrow? If either is the case, ask "what about it?" again and come up with another answer. If nothing is forthcoming, start writing. As long as you have an idea of what your topic is, you can leave the formulation of your thesis statement till later. However, if you get your thesis statement at the outset, you'll be halfway home. A well-worded thesis statement, as we'll see shortly, serves as a springboard for the work to come and both directs and helps organize the paper it heads.

FOLLOWING THROUGH

Just as tennis or golf calls for a player to follow through on a stroke, writing calls for the writer to follow through on the thesis statement—on what it implies and/or what it says overtly. To put this the other way round, if you begin with a clear thesis statement and understand what it commits you to, then the rest of your paper should be pretty much laid out. Consider in this regard the three sample thesis statements in the last subsection and what each would commit a writer to, how each would lay out the paper to come.

1. In "The Road Not Taken," Frost expresses the dilemma we often face when it comes to making important choices.

This statement directs implicitly rather than overtly, but it nonetheless directs. What is the dilemma of the poem's speaker? That would be your first consideration if you were writing on this thesis, a consideration that would entail a close look at what Frost's speaker actually says. Then you would want to consider the why of the speaker's dilemma and then, no doubt, what all of this means in symbolic terms (that is, the road symbolizes life's journey and the fork in the road symbolizes a choice of paths on life's journey). This movement from the literal to the figurative would lead seamlessly to the heart of the thesis as stated—that the poem reflects something important about us, its readers. Here you would discuss, perhaps with examples from your own life, the difficulty that making life choices often involves, especially because such choices are seldom clear-cut. You could point out, too, how we often rationalize our choices, as does the speaker of "The Road Not Taken" when he says "I took the one less traveled by." Having thus returned to the poem, you could conclude with a paragraph addressed to the relationship between art (poetry, in this case) and the lives we lead—how, for instance, a poem can make us aware of what we feel and what we do. In any case, notice that the whole projected paper flows from the thesis statement once the commitment it makes is fully understood.

> 2. In their muted colors, gentle brush strokes, and calm surfaces, Monet's last paintings capture the quiet, almost mystical serenity possible to old age.

The first half of this thesis statement overtly lays out much of the projected paper, and the last half implicitly directs the rest of it. After presenting the thesis and, perhaps, giving a little history of Monet's water-lily paintings and a generalized description of them, you would take up in turn their "muted colors," their "gentle brush strokes," and their "calm surfaces," devoting a paragraph or perhaps a cluster of several paragraphs to each. In doing so, you might refer to and focus on a single painting or several paintings if you see distinctions among them. Finally, you would move into your conclusion by discussing how Monet's late style captures the "serenity possible to old age."

> 3. Nazism took hold in Germany in the 1930s for three reasons: the Versailles Treaty of 1919, the inability of the Weimar Republic to govern, and the economic conditions during the 1920s and early 1930s both within and outside of Germany.

The paper that would follow this thesis is laid out overtly and entirely. That's why this kind of a thesis is sometimes called "a thesis with a blueprint." With your thesis stated thus, you would move on to discuss the Versailles Treaty, the Weimar Republic, and the economic conditions referred to (inflation, depression) in that order, making sure to point out step by step in what way each contributed to the rise of Nazism. You might, for instance, devote several paragraphs to the Versailles Treaty, bringing up whatever you deem pertinent to your thesis as a whole, and then point out in a paragraph or two how the Versailles Treaty helped underpin Hitler's seizing power in 1933. You would then simply repeat the pattern in treating the Weimar Republic and the economic conditions of Germany and the West at large. Having done so, you would move to your conclusion—perhaps a statement about what generally can be learned from your analysis of the rise of Nazism and the conditions that made that rise possible.

All three examples demonstrate how a thesis statement can and should relate to an essay. A well-constructed thesis statement that is understood by the writer directs the writer at each turn, controlling both what is said (content) and how it is said (form, organization). This is why I say that by getting a workable thesis statement early on and thinking into it until its commitment is fully understood, you are halfway home.

But the writer must remember the given thesis at all times and state everything in terms of that thesis. Stating things in terms of a thesis is another aspect of following through. To take an example, here are the first two paragraphs of a paper in which the student was not entirely mindful of her thesis. So she keeps veering off the track, losing her train of thought and her readers alike. Note especially the instances marked with italics.

"Useless" versus Useful Knowledge

As far as I'm concerned, there is no such thing as useless knowledge. Further, I find that what people think of as useful knowledge—the kind of knowledge one needs to perform some task or other in order to earn one's daily bread—is narrowing and finally self-defeating in the absence of the kinds of knowledge that are thought of as useless in many quarters.

I'm thinking in particular of my own high-school "education." Where I went to high school, the curriculum was devoted to *certain things* to the exclusion of *everything else*. We focused on what would get us through the SATs, not on *anything we liked*.

For instance, even our English courses were centered on *basic things* like vocabulary building. *I felt extremely frustrated in high school.*

Contrast the second paragraph, especially the words italicized, with the following revision, which is more to the point simply because things here are stated in terms of the thesis about the need for more than simply useful, or practical, knowledge.

I'm thinking in particular of my high-school "education." Where I went to high school, the curriculum was devoted to *so-called "practical" subjects* to the exclusion of *subjects deemed impractical*. We focused on what would get us through the SATs, *not on what might get us through life*. For instance, even our English courses were centered on *practical skills*, like vocabulary building. *I say "even" because English is the one class in which one most expects to find "useless," really "impractical" things like novels taught, things that can teach students only such trivia as how people relate to one another, the values that make life worth living, and what a good life is. It's no wonder that* I felt extremely frustrated in high school.

Except for the one long sentence added (the next to the last), the revised paragraph is not much different from the original. But the little bit of difference makes a big difference. "Practical subjects" in the revision, for instance, keeps the revised paragraph in focus, whereas "certain things" in the original starts the blurring that only increases as the passage goes on. It's not difficult to state what you say in terms of your thesis if you keep your thesis firmly in mind. To this end, I suggest that you write your thesis statement on a slip of paper and put it right above the keyboard of your typewriter or computer. Look at it often as you write your draft. Remind yourself at every turn of what your thesis is and of its terms. By doing so, you will be better able both to make all your statements in terms of your thesis and to keep to that thesis throughout.

DECIDING WHERE TO STATE THE THESIS

Finally, where exactly in the paper should the thesis statement be placed? Should it be, perhaps, the first sentence of a paper, or should it be the last? There is no firm answer to this question. I can think of totally successful essays in which the thesis is stated in the first sentence and others in which the thesis statement is delayed until even the last sentence. Here, for example, is a student essay in which the thesis statement appears as a conclusion and therefore comes at the end of the essay.

Rushing

One Saturday afternoon last August, my boss came up to me at the end of the lunch shift to tell me that I could have the night off. I could leave at 7:00, he said. We had been busy for breakfast and lunch, but there were only a few reservations for dinner that evening at the restaurant where I wait part-time. I made a beeline for the phone to call my boyfriend, John. At about 7:15 that evening, John arrived at my house and we were off. It was August 26, and we were on our way to see the Giants against the Jets in their first preseason football game. We rushed to the stadium, almost getting killed because of our haste (I thought my stomach would never be the same), because kickoff was at 8:00 p.m. and we had to scalp tickets.

John parked the car in the first spot available and, without even noting the lot we were in, we ran to the gate. We were in luck. There was one scalper left with one last pair of tickets, on the fifty-yard line! As we paid for them, the commentator began announcing the players. On the move again, we rushed to get to our seats before the first quarter started. In doing so, I got indigestion and John twisted his ankle on the last step. Needless to say, this was not the most enjoyable game I've ever been to, even if our seats were on the fifty-yard line.

After the game, John and I searched the parking lot for over two hours before finding our car: in our haste, remember, we had forgotten to note the lot and aisle numbers. I developed a massive headache that lasted for days. The moral, if that's what it is, of this true story is that things turn out better when one takes time and makes plans.

MAUREEN DEGNAN

A thesis statement, then, can come at the very beginning of a paper or, as you see here, at the very end. Or it can come somewhere in between. In fact, a title may even constitute the thesis statement of an essay. But having noted these possibilities, I must add emphatically that all are special cases, each being dependent on the special nature of the essay in question. You should try such different ways of placing a thesis. But do so in light of the fact that most often—say, 90 percent of the time—the best place for the thesis statement is at the end of the first paragraph or paragraph cluster.

The reason a thesis statement should usually come toward the beginning is quite simple: the reader needs to know what is being argued if each paragraph after the beginning paragraph(s) is to make a point. We've seen as much when looking at "The Jaspers" (page 20), in which everything seems pointless because of the lack of a thesis statement. The beginning is usually, even if not always, the place for the thesis statement.

That granted, why shouldn't the thesis statement come at the *very* beginning? Why at the end of the first paragraph or paragraph cluster? Essays that do begin with the thesis statement usually seem abrupt. If you want to startle your reader or to seem hurried, impatient, or perhaps frazzled, then begin immediately with your thesis statement. But because you usually don't want to approach your reader so abruptly, such a beginning is not usually effective. Usually, it's best to lead your readers in from wherever they are to where you want them to be. Thus the beginning is often called the "lead-in." I might add that of all ways of beginning, the way I've just been talking about is the one and only way that will always work. All other ways are special cases and will work only under special circumstances; the *funnel*, as this kind of beginning is called because it narrows down to the thesis statement, will work whatever the circumstance.

BEGINNINGS: THE THESIS PARAGRAPH

All right. The thesis statement should usually come at the end of the beginning. But what should come before that statement? Let me say first what should not come before it. In the opening paragraph(s), *do not* explicitly argue, support, or start to develop your thesis. Your material, of course, must be related to your thesis. But if you present overt arguments here, what will you have to say as you go on? Save arguments, supports, and so forth for your middle paragraphs. That said, we still have the question before us of what you can and should do to funnel down to the thesis statement. There are a number of answers, in fact, or a number of different ways of fulfilling the primarily psychological function of the beginning—drawing the reader in and then down to the thesis statement. Though different, these ways are nevertheless analogous, and often two, three, even four come into play simultaneously. Here are the main modes of leading to the thesis, with an example of each.

Analogy

It is possible to lead to a thesis by way of an analogy, a striking comparison that touches on some aspect of the thesis it leads to.

> Everyone knows the story of the little engine that could. It seemed too small for the task it undertook—pulling a great big train over a mountain—but it succeeded because of its positive thinking ("I think I can, I think I can, I think I can") and sheer guts. Like the little engine, our varsity basketball team seems small (the average height is only 5′11″). But it has the guts to wind up on top. *All it needs is to think positively about itself. There are at least four good reasons for it to do so.*
>
> JAMES STROH

Note how easily the analogy here leads to the thesis statement, which establishes the structure of the rest of the paper with the phrase "four good reasons." The author went on to present the reasons one by one.

Contrast

Contrast (or reversal) can also be a good way to move, perhaps from something that you consider wrong to a statement (your thesis statement) of what you consider right, or from a negative to a positive way of viewing something. The first of the following paragraphs contrasts what was expected with what actually happened. The second moves from a negative view of TV to a positive view. Notice how in each paragraph the thesis seems one with the lead-in, the two smoothly drawing the reader on.

> This summer, I had the good fortune of getting the opportunity to taste high-class living—or so I thought at the outset. I was hired as a waitress in a ritzy "members only" country club on Long Island. Thinking that I would somehow acquire millions by, for instance, helping an old dowager and consequently being left her estate, or simply by marrying a member of the club, I

walked into this job with a dazzling smile. However, my fantasy was cut short, for I soon realized that *working for the rich brings no benefits at all*, much less fringe benefits.

CLAIRE McMAHON

"Terry, that TV is going to rot your mind. Shut it off and get to your homework." While growing up, I became all too familiar with these words of my mother's. Fearing that my mind might be rotting—and fearing my mother's wrath as well—I would reluctantly turn off my favorite show and dutifully do my arithmetic. Now, looking back, I disagree with my mother. I have come to believe that *television can play a positive role in a person's development*.

TERENCE MULGREW

Here is one more example of a thesis paragraph that moves by way of contrast—this one from a generally held view that the writer rejects to a contrasting view that he means to argue.

With thirty seconds left in the game, Toronto had to kill off a penalty to beat the Flyers. Marcel Demeres, the Toronto coach, screamed at his players to go out, hit hard, and bang the puck out of the zone. The crowd screamed its assent to this bad advice, which allowed the Flyers to come back and win the game. Neither the coach nor the fans understood that *it is not intimidation that kills penalties, but aggressive forechecking, instant clearing out of the front of the net, and good goal tending*.

EDWARD BENDERNAGLE

The writer went on to argue his case by analyzing the importance to hockey of each of the three things enumerated at the end of this thesis paragraph.

Anecdote

Beginning with an anecdote of some sort or with reference to some personal experience related to your thesis can be especially effective. Note that, while moving by contrast, the preceding paragraph about the hockey game also exemplifies this way of beginning, as does the following paragraph solely.

> Laughing, my sister told me that she heard our mother say to our dog in the most serious tone of voice, "Milang, don't you remember what I told you this morning? We're having company tonight. So, if you want to stay inside, you must stay out of the living room." Now, isn't that silly? Not only do dogs not understand language, but they have no memory and can't distinguish between the living room and the bedroom much less between yesterday and today. In his poem "The Animals," Edwin Muir expresses my feelings about dogs and other such creatures exactly. *Through the abstractions of "space," "time," and "language," Muir contrasts man and the rest of the animal kingdom to delineate what is human and what is not.*
>
> Siu Lau

This paragraph moves by contrast between the mother's view and the writer's as well as the poet's (analogy is also operative here). Its other kind of movement—from anecdote to thesis—is made possible by the fact that the anecdote bears directly on the thesis. The anecdote is particularly effective because it relates to the specific terms of the thesis (which the author went on to explore): space relates to the living room, time to the mother's reference to "this morning" and "tonight," and language to talking to the dog in the first place.

Here is another example of how the writer's personal experience can lead smoothly to a thesis statement.

> With every essay I write, I am faced with a serious question. What will I title the damned thing? For me, the most torturous task when it comes to writing is thinking up an effective title. After a paper is finished, I sometimes find myself sitting in my room for hours trying to think of a title that will suit my purposes and meet my moral demands. It takes hours of hard thought because a really good title, it seems to me, must satisfy two very different criteria: first, it should not mislead the reader (this is the moral demand); yet, second, it should be imaginative. In other words, *a good title should both inform and delight.*
>
> Rae Cazzola

Familiar to Unfamiliar

Another way to set up a funnel paragraph is to move from the familiar to the unfamiliar: that is, from something related to your thesis that you know your reader knows to your thesis statement, which may be new to your reader. This is an especially good set-up for a thesis that the reader may find startling or hard to accept, for it allows the reader to get his or her bearings before being asked to strike out into uncharted territory. For example, while moving by way of analogy, the paragraph on page 30 that begins with reference to the little engine that could also moves from the familiar (the story of the little engine) to the unfamiliar (the thesis about the basketball team). Here is another example of this kind of structuring:

> Almost everybody knows what it's like to have a dog or a cat. These most popular of animals populate some two-thirds of American homes. What accounts for their prevalence? I think the answer is fur: for whatever reason, people like furry creatures—perhaps because they're cuddly—even though their hair gets all over everything. But for an occasional cuddle, dog and cat owners pay a high price: they must feed their pet once or twice a day, walk the dog two or three times a day (and use a "pooper-scooper" in most cities) or clean out the litter box (ugh!), put up with scratched furniture (in the case of cats) or chewed upholstery (in the case of dogs), and live with the allergies their pets aggravate or cause. No, I'll take a snake any day. *Snakes make perfect pets.*

> ARAIS MATESICH

As we've noted, a funnel paragraph can incorporate two or more modes of structuring at once. This paragraph, for instance, moves both from the negative (in the author's view) to the positive, and from the familiar to the unfamiliar. The latter is particularly apt here because of the surprising thesis, which the student went on to argue point by point: the ease of feeding snakes as compared with the nuisance of feeding dogs and cats, the cleanliness of snakes as compared with the messiness of dogs and cats, and so forth. In other words, this thesis paragraph not only leads naturally to the thesis (because everything in the paragraph concerns pets) but also lays out the paper as a whole.

General to Particular

Finally, many essays begin with a movement from the general to the particular: from a generalization related to the thesis to the specific thesis statement.

> Well over a hundred years ago, the British philosopher John Stuart Mill defined "modern" in connection with the freedom of choice: "[H]uman beings are no longer born to their place in life," Mill observed, "but are free to employ their faculties . . . to achieve the lot which may appear to them most desirable" (143). Our lives are no longer mapped out by tradition; we have the luxury of being able to choose what college to attend, whom we'll marry, what occupation we'll pursue. But upon what grounds can we make such choices? There's the rub. Our precious freedom leaves us in a quandary: we are often reluctant to choose and then ambivalent about the choices we've made. *In "The Road Not Taken," Robert Frost dramatizes our difficulty by way of a speaker who is representative of us human beings loosed from the constraints of tradition but not comfortable with our relatively new freedom.*

Moving from the general—the condition of modernity—to the specific—one poem by Robert Frost—this paragraph both builds to a thesis and lays out the terms of inquiry of the essay to follow. Subsequent paragraphs or groups of paragraphs would concern the speaker's reluctance to choose and his ambivalence about the choice he made along with the causes—both internal and external—for his reluctance and ambivalence, the whole paper moving inevitably to a consideration of his projected rationalization at the end of the poem. (The full paper, completed as outlined here, starts on page 72.) Again, a good thesis paragraph generally opens out the paper it heads.

REVISION OF A FUNNEL PARAGRAPH

Rarely do writers get things right the first time. The manuscripts of even (or especially) the greatest writers show them revising again and again. Writing entails just too many variables for anyone to bypass rewriting and still produce something that is readable. Beginnings in particular almost always require rewriting, for the beginning of any essay is too important not to be done right. The three paragraphs that follow demonstrate rewriting in action: the first is the student's original beginning, tentative and out of focus; the second shows her revising and suggests what she was thinking in making her revisions; and the third is the beginning in its final, revised form as it headed the paper she turned in.

First Draft

It is painful and difficult to consider the all too possible consequences of the nuclear build-up. But we all must face the frightening specter that the earth could be no more. In the past, your greatest fear may have been that your parents might die and leave you alone. Now, that fear may be for your own safety and the destruction of humanity by a nuclear holocaust. Who doesn't have great difficulty with the thought of the blackness that would descend with war, the blackness of despair, the blackness of death? Blasted, raw, charred, sterile might be all that once was greening over.

Revision

It is painful and difficult to consider the all too possible consequences of the nuclear build-up. But we all must face the frightening specter that the earth could be no more. In the past, your greatest fear may have been that your parents might die and leave you alone. Now, that fear may be for your own safety and the destruction of humanity by a nuclear holocaust. Who doesn't have great difficulty with the thought of the blackness that would descend with war, the blackness of despair, the blackness of death? Blasted, raw, charred, sterile might be all that once was greening over.

Final Version

It is painful and difficult to consider the all too possible consequences of the nuclear build-up. Who doesn't have great difficulty with the thought of the blackness that would descend with war, the blackness of despair, the blackness of death? Blasted, raw, charred, sterile might be all that once was greening over. *But we all must face the frightening specter that the earth could be no more.*

MaryAnn McCarra

Two of the sentences in the first draft here are irrelevant, serving only to blur the focus. And the thesis as stated in the first draft is obscured by its position. McCarra saw both problems and revised accordingly. The final paragraph is right on target for a paper concerned with why we each must face what the consequences of a nuclear exchange would be.

The process that led to the final version of this paper is typical. First came a halting attempt at a beginning, the first draft of which needed work but was good enough for the moment to allow the student to write on and complete a first draft of the paper. Then the whole paper was revised, with special attention at some point—whether before or after the revision of the rest—paid to the beginning. That's generally how I work, too. Of course, you might work in some other way. But however you go about things, remember that beginnings are of crucial importance and that they must nearly always be hammered into shape.

EXERCISES

1. Derive a topic from each of the following subject areas. For example, architecture is a subject area, and "the style of Frank Lloyd Wright" is a possible topic. Remember that a topic may sound like a title.

    health food   literature

    economics   animal rights

    the military   the "sixties"

    movies   China

2. Now develop a thesis and a full thesis statement for each of your topics from Exercise 1. Remember that a thesis is something *about* a topic and that at least one complete sentence is required to express a thesis. For instance, an adequate thesis statement about the style of Frank Lloyd Wright might be this: The style of Frank Lloyd Wright, with its flat planes and horizontal lines, reflects the heartland of America, the great flat expanses of the Midwest, where Wright was born and grew up.

3. Take two or three of your thesis statements from Exercise 2 and construct a funnel paragraph for each, a paragraph that leads down to the thesis statement (placed at the end of the paragraph). Pick one of the ways of funneling discussed and exemplified in this chapter—a different way (or possibly combination of ways) for each paragraph—and then follow through. Specify the strategy chosen for each of your paragraphs.

4. Now write a short paper (four or five paragraphs), with one of your thesis paragraphs from Exercise 3 (choose the one you like the best) providing the beginning. Before you begin, think about your thesis statement and determine what it commits you to, what procedure it suggests, and what you must do to support it. Then, keeping your thesis in mind at all times, write your paper in light of your thesis statement. Of course, you might have to revise your thesis—in part or even entirely—in terms of your paper as a whole once you have a first draft in hand; and you will probably have to revise the body of your paper as you check everything in it against your thesis statement. So revise, adjusting the paper to the thesis and/or the thesis to the paper, and stating everything in terms of the thesis once it's finalized.

Organization I: Fundamentals

All writing is divided into three parts: the beginning, the middle, and the end. We have spent a chapter on beginnings because beginnings are especially important and especially difficult. We shall spend another chapter (Chapter 4) on middle paragraphs and endings. First, however, we must take up certain fundamentals of organization that bear on all three parts of a composition, but particularly on middle paragraphs (the bulk of any paper) both in and of themselves and in their relationship one to the other. This chapter, then, is meant as a foundation for what we'll consider in Chapter 4.

TRANSITION

The word *transition* refers to anything in a written text that (1) demarcates the points of an argument, thereby signaling a progression from one point to the next, and (2) simultaneously glues material together, sentence to sentence and paragraph to paragraph. Transitions accomplish these two goals by showing how the parts of a composition are related. The words and phrases in italic type in the rest of this paragraph, *for instance*, are all transitional. Sometimes, *of course*, the relationship between sentences or paragraphs is self-evident, *and so* nothing additional is needed to make the relationship clear. More often, *however*, something is needed—a word, a phrase, a sentence or two, or even a whole paragraph in longer essays—for the reader to understand exactly what the writer had in mind. *Once again*, you must remember your audience. As you read a draft of a paper, put yourself in the position of your readers. *That is*, put out of mind what you intended to say and read what you actually have said, checking that the relationships between sentences and paragraphs are clear. If they are not, then provide whatever is necessary to make them so. From the reader's perspective, writing that lacks the necessary transitions is simply unreadable. As a reader yourself, you probably would not persevere through somebody else's writing if you had to supply the necessary linkages between ideas. *Besides,* readers can't be trusted to get things right. *And, in any case,* it's up to the writer to get things right in the first place.

We have already had a good example of writing that is unreadable because of the lack of transitions (as well as the lack of a thesis statement) in "The Jaspers" (Chapter 2). By examining a revision of this paper, we can see clearly what transitions are and do. On the left is the original paper, with a line through everything deleted in the revision; on the right is the writer's revision, with everything added italicized.

The Jaspers

1

~~First of all you might be wondering,~~ "What is a Jasper?" ~~We get our~~ name from a man named Jasper, who was the head of athletics at Manhattan College a number of years ago. ~~What is a Jasper today?~~ A Jasper is anyone who contributes to the college community. A Jasper is anyone who goes to Manhattan College.

What is a Jasper? *Broadly, a Jasper--the name comes* from a man named Jasper, who was the head of athletics at Manhattan College a number of *years ago--is anyone who goes to Manhattan College. More meaningfully defined,* a Jasper is *someone* who contributes to the college community. [This, now, is the thesis statement.]

2

~~Many students are avid athletes~~ whether they are ~~in~~ league or intramural ~~sports.~~ The crosscountry and the track teams ~~do extremely well each year.~~ The Lady J's basketball team ~~is also a very impressive team.~~ Swimming ~~is~~

Student athletes, for instance, contribute much to the spirit of the college. They do so whether they are *on such* league teams *as* the cross-country and track teams, the Lady J's basketball team, *the* swimming team, and the a team ~~that holds its own each year.~~ The men's basketball team ~~has a long way to go, baby. Club~~ basketball ~~does well. Club sports such as~~ golf, tennis, football, volleyball, and hockey ~~can be fun. The gym is open for those who would like to run, take an aerobics class, swim, or organize their own game.~~

There are many other extracurricular activities~~, such as:~~ Social Action, Amnesty International, Young Republicans, Young Democrats, Peace Club, Student Government, Folk Singers' Club. ~~And it is always possible for anyone to start a club.~~

Honor societies ~~reward excellent students. There are general excellence and individual honor societies.~~ The activities of ~~honor societies~~ range from printing a journal to sponsoring a speaker. ~~The school sponsors many mixers, movies, and cultural events. There are two semi-formals held each year, the Jasper Jingle and the Spring Fling. Se-~~

men's basketball team; or such intramural <u>teams as</u> basketball, golf, tennis, football, volleyball, and hockey. <u>All such students deserve the name "Jasper."</u>

3   There are many other extracurricular activities <u>through which a student can participate in campus life. They include</u> Social Action, Amnesty International, Young Republicans, Young Democrats, Peace Club, Student Government, Folk Singers' Club. <u>Those who join such clubs are true Jaspers.</u>

4   <u>Those students elected to</u> honor societies, the activities of <u>which</u> range from printing a journal to sponsoring a speaker, <u>equally deserve the name "Jasper." For they, too, contribute.</u>

~~nior week is a special~~
~~time for seniors. It is~~
~~filled with a variety of~~
~~activities, from the hon-~~
~~ors convention to the~~
~~prom.~~

Of course, who could   5   Of course, who could
be a Jasper without going   be a Jasper without going
to the bars below campus   to the bars below campus
on Broadway now and again?   on Broadway now and again?
~~All of~~ this ~~and so much~~   This, <u>too, defines what</u> a
~~more make~~ a Jasper.   Jasper <u>is.</u>

To be sure, this revision entails more than the addition of transitions. The first paragraph has been rewritten so that it funnels to a thesis, which is then developed throughout the rest of the paper, paragraph by paragraph. Also, everything that is irrelevant to the thesis as it now stands has been deleted. Both the additions and the deletions give the revised paper focus and point. But, most of all, observe how coherence is gained, how transitions clarify the relationships of the sentences and paragraphs in the revision:

Paragraph 1:   *Broadly* and *more meaningfully defined* are transitional. In relation to each other, they structure the paragraph and bring its ideas into relationship.

Paragraph 2:   *For instance* relates the first and second paragraphs and gives the second paragraph point. Taken together, *on such* and *or such* provide transition as they help to structure the paragraph.

Paragraph 3:   The word "other" is the key transition here, linking paragraphs 2 and 3 by suggesting that paragraph 3 is an extension of 2.

Paragraph 4:   *Equally* and *too* are both transitional, relating paragraphs 2 and 3 to paragraph 4 and thereby giving point to paragraph 4.

Paragraph 5:   Here, again, *too* is transitional, relating the last paragraph to the rest of the paper.

Transition, then, frequently can be attained simply by the addition of a word or short phrase. The most common are conjunctive adverbs and subordinating conjunctions. The former include such words or phrases as *however, therefore, consequently, moreover, thus, also, besides, furthermore, nevertheless, still, for example,* and *for instance.* Notice that each shows a specific kind of relationship: *for instance* says that what follows is a specific case of a generalization stated before; *however* and *nevertheless* show contrary movement; and *therefore, thus,* and *consequently* all say that what follows is a result of what precedes. Subordinating conjunctions also show relationship. *Because,* for example, shows a cause-and-effect relationship between what is said in the main clause of a sentence and what is said in the subordinate clause that it (the subordinating conjunction *because*) heads; *although* shows a contrary relationship between main and subordinate clauses; words like *after* and *when* show a time relationship; and *if* and *unless* say that what is said in the clause headed by the one or the other is a condition for what is stated in the main clause.

Consider the following sentences and their revisions, in which things are clearly tied together by subordinating conjunctions and conjunctive adverbs:

Molly said she wants you to stay home. She wants you to watch the baby. I can't take you with me.

Molly said that she wants you to stay home *because* she wants you to watch the baby. *Therefore,* I can't take you with me.

Harry was late. He got to his seat just before the curtain went up. The play was over. He was left with many feelings. He felt sad and yet somehow elated.

Although Harry was late, he got to his seat just before the curtain went up. *When* the play was over, he was left with many feelings. *For instance,* he felt sad and yet somehow elated.

Many other words and phrases can also serve as transitions. For example, in the revision of "The Jaspers," as we've seen, the adjective *other* and the adverb *equally* both are transitional. The seven coordinating conjunctions, too, are transitional, each showing a specific kind of relationship: *and* (similarity), *but* and *yet* (contrast), *for* and *so* (result, cause and effect), *or* (equivalence or alternate possibility), and *nor* (equality in negation).

Repetition of a word or phrase from one sentence to the next can also effect transition, as can the use of pronouns because they refer back to a noun or proper name used earlier:

> It is clear, then, that women were essential during the colony's first year; that they remained essential during the years to come can be just as easily shown.

Often a whole sentence or even a whole paragraph might be transitional. For instance, let's say that you're going to write a short paper on the Pilgrims, your thesis falling into two parts—first, that the female Pilgrims were essential for the survival of the colony in its first year here and, second, that they continued to be essential thereafter. After your thesis paragraph, you might devote a paragraph to the first half of the thesis, supporting it with whatever evidence you could bring to bear. Then, you would tackle the second half of the thesis in your third paragraph. But how would you get from the one to the other? A full sentence at the start of the third paragraph would probably be needed, something like the sample sentence just given ("It is clear, then, that . . .").

Having finished your argument and written a conclusion, you would have a short paper in hand. But, now, say that you are going to write a much longer paper with the same thesis, with five or six paragraphs devoted to the first part of the thesis and an equal number to the second. In this case, you might need a short transitional paragraph between the two segments of the paper, a paragraph something like this:

> There is no question, then, that women were essential to the survival of the colony during its first year. As I've shown, it was the women, and not the Pilgrim Fathers, who knew how to find and prepare the roots and berries that fed the colony during that long first winter. But women also remained essential to the colony after its first year in America. So now let us turn to the later history of the Pilgrim Mothers.

This whole paragraph would be transitional, serving to link the two halves of the paper and to make it one.

Transitions—whether a word or a phrase, a sentence or a paragraph—are a mark of thoughtful (in both senses of the word) and mature writing. Linking sentences as well as larger segments within paragraphs, linking paragraphs as well as larger divisions of a piece of writing, transitions more than anything else make writing readable. While demarcating points, they serve as signposts that tell the reader where the writer is going; they help structure a piece of writing and at the same time reveal to the reader how it is structured and so keep the reader from getting lost. Thus, transition and organization go hand in glove. Comprehensible organization requires transitions, and that's all there is to it.

To be sure, as we have noted, sometimes the relationship between sentences and paragraphs is self-evident, and so nothing additional is needed to make the relationship clear. That's the ideal—writing that is seamless, organic, coherent by nature, or at least seemingly so. With regard to the movement of its paragraphs, the following paper is an excellent example.

Three Months with the Aboto

Having lived among Southwest Africa's Aboto people for three months, I have learned much about them. First, they are a harmless people who subsist on the vegetation and animals around them. Second, they are literal communists, sharing everything they have with each other and doing whatever they do for the good of the tribe. And third, though close knit, the Aboto welcome strangers and coexist peacefully with the many white settlers who surround their territory.

Peaceful hunters and gatherers, Aboto men and women go off each morning in separate directions to find food. The women gather grasses, nuts, and berries, while the men hunt down wild boars and iguanas. Hunting, however, is the only aggressive action allowed in the tribe. On my first day with the Aboto, I was given one rule: violence is never permissible; violence of any kind leads automatically to expulsion from the Aboto land.

Absence of aggression between tribal members fosters tribal unity. "I am because we are, and because we are, I am" is the creed by which every Aboto lives—lives peacefully with his or her fellows. Like a well-oiled machine of many parts, the tribe works because of this sense of unity. Everyone contributes to the life of the community and everything is shared by all. As a result of their creed, the Aboto have survived in the Southwest African wilds for many centuries.

Although the Aboto are close knit, they are not closed-minded when dealing with strangers. In the past eighty years, French, English, and Dutch settlers have settled in territories that surround Aboto land. And never once has there been trouble between the settlers and these peaceful hunter-gatherers. The Aboto-Ka (tribal elder) told me that as long as "the pale ones" act the way human beings should, the Aboto are content to live next to them.

I myself was received most warmly by these people. When I arrived at their main village, I was immediately surrounded by laughing children. And when, over the first meal I was given, I revealed that my plan was to study them by day while spending my nights at one of the settlements, they immediately invited me to live with them so as to get to know them better than a daytime guest ever could. My three-month stay with the Aboto and as an Aboto was one of the best periods of my life. To be sure, the work was hard and the sun was hot. But such things pale to nothing when one feels that, as we say in Aboto, "Kwe-Ha"—life is good.

TRACY MASUCCI

In part, the thesis paragraph and the author's follow-through on it account for the structural tightness of this essay: the three statements of the thesis paragraph—clearly labeled "first," "second," and "third"—are taken up in order in paragraphs 2, 3, and 4–5. No transitions between paragraphs are needed, for the material is handled in a way that makes transitions unnecessary. How so? Well, paragraph 2 ends with the thought that "violence is never permissible"; paragraph 3 concerns the "absence of aggression." The one easily leads to the other, the two paragraphs being related by similarity. Paragraph 3 also concerns the "unity" of the tribe; paragraph 4, in contrast, concerns the tribe's openness to people of other cultures. The relationship here is self-evidently that of contrast. Paragraph 5 continues the subject of paragraph 4, but on a personal level; and the last paragraph winds things up. There are no loose ends here; everything fits together as tightly as pieces in a jigsaw puzzle.

But don't mistake me. What I have just been talking of is the ideal, which, to be sure, you should strive for. Generally speaking, however, transitions are necessary to show the reader how you're getting from *a* to *b*. Sometimes, there's magic in the air and what you're writing comes out all of a piece, without overt linkage. But most of the time, the writer has to provide words, phrases, sentences, or whole paragraphs to make the transition and bring the reader along on the stream of an essay's thought.

UNITY AND COHERENCE

In Chapter 1 I stated that the primary business of rewriting is to make sure that everything is to the point and follows as logically and gracefully as possible. In other words, a finished piece of writing should be both unified and coherent, unity and coherence being intimately related to transition and organization. Prose that does not show unity and coherence is like the rambling of one of those radio talk-show callers who go on and on aimlessly and never really make a point at all. They are painful to listen to, just as the original version of "The Jaspers" is painful to read, lacking as it does both unity (because much in it is irrelevant) and coherence (because nothing relates to anything else). Readers, too, want the writer to make a point and stick to it by relating all supporting points both to the main point and to each other. The first is a matter of unity; the second, of coherence.

To be more specific, unity means that everything in a paper somehow points back to and supports the governing thesis—the thesis, note, and not merely the topic. We might think of the relationship of thesis and supporting material as being vertical:

Thesis

Supporting Sentences and Paragraphs

But what if something is not related vertically to the thesis? You can rewrite to gain unity in one of several ways. First, and most obvious, anything that seems irrelevant, and so breaks the sense of unity, can be deleted. For example, the second sentence of the following passage is totally irrelevant as stated and therefore destroys the sense of unity and coherence as well:

> Standardized tests do not really measure one's abilities. The most hated tests are the ones from our friends in Princeton. Standardized tests do not measure one's abilities, but only one's test-taking skills.

What does the fact that the SATs (which come from Princeton, New Jersey) are hated have to do with the thesis that standardized tests don't really measure one's abilities? Nothing. After all, tests that do successfully measure abilities might well be equally hated. No necessary relationship exists between the two statements, and none is drawn as the passage stands. The two derive from the same topic, of course, but remember that everything in a paper must relate to its specific thesis and not merely to its general topic. One way to revise is simply to delete the second sentence:

> Standardized tests do not really measure one's abilities. These exams measure only one's test-taking skills.

Now there is nothing extraneous; now the passage has unity.

Another way to revise for unity is to take anything that is irrelevant as stated and to state it in terms of the thesis. We've had an example of this kind of revision already (page 27), which you may want to look back to, but here let's stay with the sample about standardized testing. The second sentence of the original passage could be retained by restating it thus:

> Standardized tests do not really measure one's abilities. Certainly, those most hated tests from our friends in Princeton don't. All these and other such tests measure is one's test-taking skills.

Yet another way of gaining unity—one, indeed, suggested by the last revision (in which "our friends in Princeton" is subordinated)—is subordination. Disunity and incoherence typically result from putting every thought into an independent clause or sentence. Only prime information should go into prime positions; all else should be subordinated by being put into a phrase or a subordinate clause:

Standardized tests, like those most hated tests from our friends at Princeton, do not really measure one's abilities. All such tests measure are one's test-taking skills.

Here, the business about the "most hated tests" as well as about "our friends in Princeton" is put into a prepositional phrase, the preposition in each phrase acting as a link (a transition) from thought to thought. To be sure, one usually finds some material that got into one's first draft that is simply irrelevant and must be deleted. Often, however, a sentence that breaks unity because of the way it is stated can be salvaged by restatement in terms of the thesis or by subordination. At other times, the point of a sentence or a paragraph must be spelled out so that its relationship to the thesis is clear. For example, the second paragraph of the revision of "The Jaspers" (page 39), the one beginning with a statement about student athletes' contributing to the college followed by a list of athletic teams, ends with an overt statement of the point: "All such students deserve the name 'Jasper.'" The statement is needed to ensure that the reader will see how what is said in the paragraph is related to the thesis.

A passage that lacks unity will also lack coherence. But coherence is different from unity, as is suggested by the fact that it is quite possible to write a unified paper that is incoherent. Unity, as we've seen, is a matter of vertical relationship, or the relation of everything in a paper to its thesis. Coherence, on the other hand, is a matter of horizontal relationship, or the relation of every sentence and every paragraph to what comes before and after:

$$\longrightarrow \quad \longleftrightarrow \quad \longleftrightarrow \quad \longleftrightarrow \quad \longleftrightarrow \quad \longleftrightarrow \quad \longleftarrow$$

So I sometimes have occasion to say to one of my students, "Yes, all of your sentences and paragraphs relate to your thesis. But how do they relate to each other?" Here's a quick example of what I mean:

The summer of 1989 is over, but not forgotten. Once again, I spent my vacation at the Jersey shore with my friends and relatives. The highlight of many teenage girls' first day back is finding out which lifeguards have returned for another season. Lifeguards go on duty at 8 a.m.

The first two sentences are all right, linked, as they are, by the phrase "once again." The second two, however, are badly incoherent, both in

relationship (or lack thereof) to each other and to the sentences that begin the passage. What to do? Well, you could try subordination, thereby
grammatically expressing the relationship of the two ideas:

> The highlight of many teenage girls' first day back is finding out
> which lifeguards have returned for another season, even though that
> means getting up before 8 a.m., when the lifeguards go on duty.

You can also achieve coherence by overtly explaining how a supporting idea or fact relates to another supporting idea or fact if the relationship is not obvious. And, most of all, you can achieve coherence by using
transitions, whose sole purpose is to spell out the kind of relationship that
exists between sentences and paragraphs when that relationship is not
self-evident (and it usually is not). The lack of coherence between the
second and third sentences of the sample passage can be corrected by
these two means:

> The summer of 1989 is over, but not forgotten. Once again, I
> spent my vacation at the Jersey shore with my friends and relatives.
> And once again [transition], the highlight of many teenage girls' first
> day back proved to be finding out which lifeguards had returned for
> another season, even though that meant getting up before 8 a.m.,
> when the lifeguards go on duty. As usual, I was one of those girls.
> [spelling out]

Finally, coherence can be gained by simply restating a sentence to
incorporate something from the preceding sentence or from the thesis
itself. For instance, the incoherence of the first pair of sentences that
follows is easily rectified by the italicized addition in the second pair:

> The psychological and emotional scars of divorce are traumatic and
> long-lasting. A child who is witness to a constant bombardment of
> violent arguments is apt to be left with the warped impression that
> such arguments are normal.

> The psychological and emotional scars of divorce can be traumatic
> and long-lasting. A child who is witness to the constant bombard-
> ment of violent arguments *that almost always precedes a divorce* is
> apt to be left with the warped impression that such arguments are
> normal.

Every sentence within a paragraph, then, and every paragraph in a paper must somehow relate both to the thesis and to the previous sentence or paragraph and the following sentence or paragraph. And if one or another element doesn't so relate, then incoherence looms and the reader is sure to get lost. When writing and especially when rewriting, therefore, watch that the relationship of your sentences and paragraphs is clear at all points. And if at any point it isn't clear, then subordinate, supply a transition, explain yourself in a sentence or two, restate, or delete. You might also try doing what I do—indeed, I urge you to. When I write, I look back and back again: I seldom write a sentence without rereading the sentence before it, nor do I usually begin a paragraph without reviewing at least the end of the preceding paragraph. In this way, I get my brain into the groove of coherence, as it were, and create the situation whereby sentence gives rise to sentence, paragraph to paragraph. Coherence, thus, is all but assured, though in the rewriting stage I still check that what I've written is coherent and make the necessary adjustments when needed. In fact, I made one such adjustment in revising the paragraph you are now reading by adding the sentence "You might also try doing what I do—indeed, I urge you to" a few sentences back. On rereading, I felt that there was a gap at that point, that I had jumped from thought to thought and left the reader behind. Linking what comes before to what comes after, the added sentence fills that gap.

Although "The Jaspers," or its revision, well illustrates what I've been saying, one more example wouldn't hurt. The contrast between the original paragraphs and the revision that follows should underscore the difference between writing that seems aimless because it lacks unity and coherence and writing that, because it is unified and coherent, stays to a point and makes it. Note especially the coherent movement from the first to the second paragraph in the rewrite as opposed to the incoherence from paragraph to paragraph of the original. Both drafts concern Frost's "The Road Not Taken," which you might reread before going on (see page 4).

Original

Robert Frost is a great poet. We studied the poem "The Road Not Taken" in high school. Robert Frost is known as having been an individualist. That's what my teacher said the poem is about. You have to go away from the beaten path and make a path of your own.

I thought it was okay. What my teacher said seemed okay. I liked the last two lines.

We studied the poem in college. It means something else. The poem is about the difficulty of making important choices. Often, there's nothing much to go on. His speaker is ambivalent. He focuses not on the road taken but on the one not taken. He says "sigh" and "all the difference" without telling us what kind of sigh or difference. A choice can be very hard to make. We never know how things will turn out. I had a lot of trouble choosing a college. I know what he means.

Rewrite

Deletion & Subordination	<u>When</u> we studied Robert Frost's poem "The Road Not Taken" in high school, we were told
Subordination	that Frost was a "rugged individualist" <u>whose</u> poem concerns individualism—<u>that is,</u> going away from the beaten path and making a path of one's
Transition	own. <u>That interpretation</u> seemed good to me at
Subordination	the time <u>because</u> in the last line the poet says
Deletion & Polishing	(or seems to say) right out, "I took the one less traveled by."
Transition between ¶'s	<u>Now, however,</u> I believe the poem is about something else. <u>Having studied</u> it again in college,
Subordination	I think that Frost is getting at the diffi-
Subordination	culty of making important choices <u>when</u> there is nothing much to go on. What makes me think
Transition	<u>this</u> is the speaker's ambivalence throughout the poem about the choice he made, his ambivalence
Subordination	<u>being suggested</u> especially by his focusing on the road <u>not</u> taken and his regretting having to leave it behind. His ambivalence is a token of
Transition	his difficulty. <u>Then, too,</u> he does not tell us
Transition	that he made the right choice: <u>certainly,</u> the words "sigh" (line 16) and "difference" (line 20) could indicate something negative just as
Transition	well as something positive. <u>These</u> ambiguities suggest that we have difficulty making choices
Subordination	<u>because</u> we cannot know beforehand how things

Transitions
Subordination

Transition

> will turn out, whether for the better or the
> worse. <u>How true this is. For instance,</u> I had
> terrible trouble choosing a college <u>because</u> I
> couldn't determine which one would be best for
> me; <u>that is,</u> I couldn't know at the outset what
> I needed to know to make the right choice. I,
> for one, know what Frost means. His poem is mean-
> ingful because it reflects common experience.

The first set of paragraphs lacks coherence from the second sentence on. And the first sentence lacks unity. In the revision, the first sentence is deleted because, even though it may be true, it is irrelevant. The second sentence as stated relates to neither the first nor the third sentences. In fact, none of the sentences in the first paragraph show anything like a clear relationship. The reader is left to decipher what possible connections there could be; few readers would even try. Everything seems to come from left field. To be sure, all of the sentences relate more or less to Frost and/or "The Road Not Taken"—that is, to the topic area and/or topic. But none relate to a thesis, much less to each other. Look, now, at the first revised paragraph. Because irrelevant (and, thus, disunified), the first and sixth sentences of the original have simply been deleted; the second through the fifth sentences have been combined—and thereby made coherent—by way of subordination; the seventh and eighth sentences have been combined by subordination, linked to the now-first sentence by a transitional phrase and polished by specification. Similar problems mark the second paragraph of the original, and similar solutions are found in its revised counterpart. But observe especially the transition at the beginning of the second revised paragraph and the difference in clarity that the transition makes. Almost any piece of writing can be made unified and coherent if the writer spots what is needed in this regard and then does it.

BASIC PATTERNS OF ORGANIZATION

We have been considering what might be called "micro" coherence—that is, the relating of sentences and paragraphs to one another. But the writer must also be aware of "macro" coherence, of the larger coherences of paragraphs and papers overall. In the rest of this chapter, we shall look at five basic patterns of organization of paragraphs and papers alike. The examples here will all be paragraphs; in the next chapter we will see the patterns in complete papers.

Chronology

Whenever something occurs over a period of time, you can write about it in chronological sequence. That is, in describing or analyzing an event, for instance, you could arrange your material according to the sequence of the event itself as the event actually unfolded in time. Whatever happened first comes first, what happened second comes second, and so forth. Perhaps the most psychologically ingrained of patterns, chronological sequence is a particularly easy way of organizing once its possibility is recognized. All the writer must do is follow the sequence of what is being written about, making sure that the sequence is clear by providing time markers (transitions) between each of its segments. Here is an example of a paragraph organized chronologically, with all transitions put in italics (as will be all transitions in all of the sample paragraphs to follow).

> *Not long ago*, I found myself ambling down Fifth Avenue. I had no place in particular to go, so I just took in the sights as I took my time. *Then*, something happened to change the character of my day: as I casually watched the cars going by, a woman in a fur coat darted out into the traffic mid-block and was struck by a green Mercedes. I stuck around because, though there were hundreds of people on both sides of the street, I was the only one, it seemed, who had actually witnessed the accident. In any case, the police arrived *shortly after* the accident, and *maybe a half an hour later* an ambulance appeared. *By then*, however, it was too late: the woman had died a good *ten minutes earlier*. *Once* she had been hauled off, the police told me to come to the station to make a report. *After that*, I went home, arriving *late* for dinner but fed up with the world. *Now*, *when* I reflect on the incident, I can only think of all of those people and me the only witness.

MARY PAT BURKE

Spatial Sequence

Whenever something being written about exists in space or can be thought of in terms of physical extension, spatial sequence can be a good way of organizing: left to right or right to left, upward or downward, inward or outward, far to near or near to far, and so on. For instance, the sequence might be first a distanced view of something from the outside, then a closer view, and then a shot of the inside (this sequence being far to near). The point is that the order of first to second to third cannot be random; every paragraph and every essay must proceed by a plan, which must be clear to the reader. Thus, a spatial sequence, like a chronological sequence, must have markers between segments that make the sequence clear. Now, however, the transitions will be spatial in character rather than temporal.

> *From a distance of a few hundred yards*, the old Newberry castle, which sits atop a rather steep hill, seems like something out of Camelot. With its turrets and terraces, it looks as splendid as it must have looked in its heyday at the turn of the century. *Even from a few hundred feet* the castle keeps its secret, like an aging movie star in a veil. But *close up* it shows its age. Because of years of neglect, its slate shingles have become loose and many have fallen; most of its window panes are cracked or missing; and its cement balustrades and gargoyles, some of which lie on the ground, have eroded and decayed. *Inside*, the story is the same. The place is a shambles. But *from a few hundred yards away*, it still looks like a castle where King Arthur might be presiding over the round table.
>
> ALFRED J. REINER

Comparison and Contrast

Comparison and contrast offers a prime way of understanding: in everyday life we frequently come to grasp something by seeing how it is like and/or unlike something else. No less is true when we write. For the writer, comparison and contrast is a tool of analysis that also provides ways in which a paragraph or a whole paper can be organized.

Technically, comparison emphasizes similarity and contrast emphasizes difference. In practice, however, the distinction is not so clear-cut, for comparison involves contrast and contrast entails comparison. This is so because what usually makes a comparison meaningful is that the like things being compared actually have some significant difference, and what gives a contrast point is that the unlike things being contrasted actually share some fundamental likeness.

We can organize comparisons and contrasts in a number of ways. The two most common are *point by point* (A/B, A/B, A/B—or some variant) and *blocked* (all of A and then all of B, with the comparison/contrast drawn in the B block). The following paragraphs show these two ways of organizing.

Point by Point

Stainless and sterling flatware are alike in many ways. Obviously, they look alike as to form: forks, knives, spoons have the same shape whatever they're made of. *Also*, a set of good stainless can be just about as attractive on a table as sterling. *Further*, both wear well: silver flatware can be handed down for generations, and stainless is practically indestructible. *However*, stainless lacks the two most wonderful qualities of silver: its heft in the hand and its silkiness on the lips. *Finally*, therefore, there is no comparison at all.

Blocked

Stainless steel makes a fine material for flatware. It is cheap, it can be brought to a high polish, and it is almost indestructible. *Further*, it is dishwasher safe and never needs polishing. Yes, for most people's daily needs, stainless is the flatware of choice. *In contrast with* stainless, sterling silver is expensive and is not dishwasher safe. *Moreover, unlike* stainless, sterling needs to be polished frequently and stored carefully so that the sulfur in the air doesn't get at it. *To be sure*, sterling has a wonderful heft and silkiness that stainless lacks, and sterling is also durable. The two are alike, *then*, in having both pluses and minuses. One's choice must depend on one's circumstance and inclinations.

The first sample moves point by point, from a consideration of both stainless and sterling as to form, then attractiveness, then durability, and it ends with two crucial points of difference. The second sample moves from a discussion of various features of stainless, considered in a block, to a discussion of contrasting features of sterling, considered in another block. The paragraph ends with a likeness, which serves to give the contrast point.

These two basic ways of making a comparison/contrast can also work in combination: for instance, one paragraph constructed point by point and the next blocked. And we can structure a comparison/contrast in other ways as well. One that is quite elegant but hard to pull off is to discuss all of A in and of itself and—making sure to provide a bridge—all of B in and of itself, and then move to the comparison/contrast in the next section. Keeping to our comparison/contrast of stainless and sterling, you could discuss everything you have to say about stainless first; then, bridging with a statement like "Of course, many people prefer sterling silver," you could go on to discuss the merits of sterling. Then you could move to the point of the comparison/contrast in a C block.

In deciding among these various ways of handling a comparison/contrast, you should consider the effect you desire along with the projected length of what you are writing. If you wish your pace to be quick, use the point-by-point type of arrangement; if you wish your pace to be more leisurely, use the block type. If you are writing a longish paper, it might be best to move point by point, each paragraph or paragraph cluster concerning one point of comparison or contrast (for a block organization in a longer paper runs the risk that readers will forget what is said in the paragraphs that constitute the A block by the time they get to the B block); if the paper is to be short, however, then blocking might be ideal, as might the A-B-C kind of structure.

Whichever of these strategies you choose, what should come first, what second, what third, and so on is still a pressing consideration. Let's say that you have decided to move point by point, A/B, A/B, A/B. But which A/B will you put first, which second, which third? This decision should stem as much as possible from the material at hand. If what you are writing about is temporal or spatial, say, then the points in your comparison/contrast could be arranged accordingly. For instance, comparing Western and Eastern values, you might move chronologically, taking up ancient values first, then values from the Middle Ages and Renaissance, and then modern values. (Note that the various ways of organizing considered here often overlap, with two or more ways working together to lend structure and coherence.) Or order of climax—the last mode of organizing we'll consider in this chapter—might provide a rationale. Whatever the case, you should have a reason for the order you choose and you must somehow make the reader aware of that reason.

Enumeration

In enumerating, the writer lists in the thesis statement the points to be made in the paragraph or paper to follow, or at least suggests that a certain number of points will be taken up, and then goes on to develop them one by one. Accordingly, some typical series of transitions that enumeration calls for are these:

first, second, third, finally

to begin with, then, then again, last

at first, however, then, third, and finally

The following sample paragraph well exemplifies enumeration.

> According to E. M. Forster in his essay "My Wood," there are four reasons why property is dangerous to the soul. *In the first place*, property makes one pompous and spiritually stout. In support of this contention, Forster argues that "Property produces men of weight," that is, people who are self-important and self-satisfied. *Then*, property tends to make one "avaricious": even a little bit of property tends to foster a desire for more and more. *Third*, ownership leads to a "pseudo-creativity," like the maintaining of lawns in the suburbs (my example), and, thus, leads away from genuine creativity and life-affirming values. *Last, and most important*, owning property makes one "intensely selfish." "Keep off the Grass," "Keep Out," "Private Property"—these are the property owner's mottos. Indeed, Forster's very title reflects this fourth charge if we hear the stress on the first word: "*My* Wood." It is no wonder that, quoting Dante, Forster concludes that "'Possession is one with loss.'"

> MARGE MARKEY

We move from part to part here by way of transitions appropriate to enumeration. But why the order of the four parts—spiritual stoutness to avariciousness to pseudo-creativity to selfishness? Again, the writer should always have a reason for ordering parts as they are ordered. Like comparison/contrast, enumeration can incorporate a chronological or spatial sequence to order points if either is possible. For instance, a thesis statement concerning the four interesting sights to see on the way from Cleveland to St. Louis could proceed by enumeration with the points ordered spatially: *first along the road, then we come to, third, about five hundred miles further, finally, almost at the door of St. Louis*. As to the sample paragraph, its points follow the order of Forster's points in his essay. (In writing about literature, often all you need to do is follow the sequence of the story, poem, or essay under consideration.) But why did Forster arrange the parts of his essay thus? The answer is suggested in the sample paragraph by the phrase "Last and most important." Forster's essay moves from point to point in an order of climax, our last category of organization.

Order of Climax

I've saved order of climax—that is, building to the most important point—for last because of its special importance. Climactic arrangement is particularly important because it applies to all other ways of organizing. Should you be enumerating, for instance, or comparing and contrasting, order of climax could help you decide how to arrange the parts of your composition, the most important always coming last. Even chronological and spatial sequences, though having their own sequential logic, can move climactically (for instance, from a cause in the past to its subsequent result; or from a false appearance at a distance to the reality up close). And should your material suggest no other kind of order, remember that climactic order is always possible: simply decide which of your points is the most important, which the least, and which in between; then arrange the parts accordingly—that is, from least to most important—making sure to include transitions that let your reader know how you are proceeding. But even if you are working with some other pattern, keep order of climax in mind. If for no other reason than to avoid the silliness of anticlimax (as in "He ran off with my wife and dented my car"), check for order of climax as you arrange parts into paragraphs and then paragraphs into an essay. The last sample paragraph of this chapter shows how order of climax can structure material that does not suggest innately any other kind of order. As you read the paragraph, observe how the writer uses transitional phrases to mark his various points and to make clear how the material is organized.

Of the many ill effects of alcohol, perhaps the *least important*—though this might sound odd at first—is its effect on the body. To be sure, alcohol rots the liver and destroys the brain. But that's the business of the individual. This is a free country, and the choice to destroy oneself is an individual matter. Or it would be if there were not other considerations involved. However, there are other considerations, the family being one. *More important* than what alcohol does to the individual is what it does to the family of the alcoholic. In the majority of cases, it leads to the dissolution of the alcoholic's family, with all of the misery that divorce entails, especially for children. And even if alcoholism doesn't lead finally to divorce, it still inevitably causes misery to the other family members, who are guilty only of tolerating the behavior of the drunken mother or father. *But most important by far*—at least from society's point of view—is the collective effect of alcoholism on the nation at large. Statistics show that, taken together, the nation's alcoholics significantly reduce American productivity on the one hand (because of days absent and work done shoddily) and significantly increase the cost of medical insurance and care on the other. For all of these reasons, but *especially the last*, it seems to me that we should not tolerate excessive drinking one day more.

Barry J. Gillin

EXERCISES

1. Decide what kind of transition is needed in each of the following paragraphs (for example, transitions showing contrast or an order of climax) and then supply the transitions needed where indicated by an asterisk (*).

    a. We went to town on Thursday. * we found a place to stay. * we hunted up Jake, my old college buddy. We spent a couple of hours at his place. * the three of us went out to dinner. * Nan and I went back to the hotel for a good night's sleep.

    b. Axel's Castle, in Brighton, is approached by a steep and winding road. * the castle looks like a vision. However, * the place turns out to be a ruin. Outside, it seems nothing but a mass of cracks. * it is in no better shape, what with its ceilings crumbling and its floor boards rotting away. Axel's Castle is quite dispiriting.

    c. There are four things a student needs to know to succeed in college. * is how to take notes. Good, orderly notes are essential for later study and recall. Related to the first, * is how to prepare for and take exams. Equally important is * : how to act in class. The student must understand that cross-talking and class participation affect teachers equally, though one negatively and the other positively. * and * is how to write a coherent analysis of a given subject.

For more than anything else, a student's papers show his or her intellectual level and grasp of the material at hand. Without doubt, the students who succeed in college are those students who *.

2.   Supply a transition of whatever kind seems appropriate where indicated by an asterisk (*).

Proofreading is the final stage of the writing process. * the brain cannot do everything at once, proofreading should be done in steps. * read your final draft once through, checking for subject-verb agreement errors only. * read it again, checking only for pronoun reference and agreement. All three are potential problem spots, and * they require special attention. * read your paper for spelling, punctuation, and other matters of mechanics, preferably aloud so that you can also check the sound of your prose. Watch especially for errors that you know you are prone to make. * if your writing does not sound like you, something is wrong. Go back and rephrase anything that seems stilted or roundabout.

* give your paper a title. To be sure, you may have a tentative title in mind even before you start writing. * it is best to wait until the last to make a final decision about a title for two reasons: * you can't be sure of what you're going to say until you've said it, * a title can never be more than tentative until the last; * if you wait to give your paper a title, you will not fall into an error (and it is an error) that students sometimes fall into—that is, of referring to a title in the paper itself. An * error is not to title what you have written. Be sure to give everything you write a title. Remember that a title—the first thing a reader sees—focuses the reader's attention and draws the reader in. Titles are functional * and should be chosen with care.

3.   Relate the following pairs of sentences first with an appropriate coordinating conjunction (*and, but, for, or, nor, so, yet*); then with an appropriate subordinating conjunction (choose from these—*just as, since, although, after, when, because, in the same way as, while*); and finally with a conjunctive adverb (choose from these—*consequently, however, afterwards, moreover, therefore, likewise, nonetheless, similarly, nevertheless*). You may transpose sentences if you wish, but whether or not you do, be sure to adjust the punctuation of each new construction.

a. There is no arguing with taste. Everyone is entitled to his or her own opinion.

b. The early bird catches the worm. It is the early worm that gets caught.

c. The flesh is weak. The spirit is willing.

d. He makes me lie down in green pastures. He leads me beside still waters.

e. What is good for one is good for many. One man's meat is another's poison.

f. Take no thought of tomorrow. Sufficient unto the day is the trouble thereof.

g. Pride goeth before destruction. A haughty spirit goeth before a fall.

4. Use subordination to combine the sentences of each of the following blocks into a single sentence per block. Your four final sentences should compose a paragraph that is both unified and coherent. To achieve this goal, be sure to keep the focus of each combined sentence on the writing of a term paper.

Term Paper

a. (1) A trash can sat in the corner of the room.
     (2) The trash can was filled with the pages of a term paper.
     (3) The pages had been rejected.
     (4) The room was in a dorm.

b. (1) The desk was cluttered with more papers.
     (2) And the desk was cluttered with books.
     (3) The desk was old.
     (4) The desk had initials carved in it.
     (5) The desk had obscene remarks carved in it.
     (6) The carving was by two generations of students.
     (7) The books were piled on top of each other.

c. (1) Mark's father had given him the word processor.
     (2) It was a present for graduation.
     (3) The graduation was from high school.
     (4) The word processor was portable.
     (5) It sat in the middle of the desk.

d. (1) A package of No-Doz fell to the floor.
     (2) Mark picked up the paper.
     (3) The paper was the one he had completed during the night.

5. Rewrite each of the following for unity and coherence.

My Worst Course

The course I took last term in psychology was disappointing. I'm interested in what makes people tick. I love history. The course I had seemed to be only about rats. We studied rats running mazes, rats going mad in deprivation chambers, rats getting electrocuted. Rats hold a certain amount of interest. Rats are not people. As I said, I love history. People are what I'm interested in. My psych course was disappointing.

Reading

Reading provides us with a way of gaining knowledge. Literature includes poems, novels, plays, and short stories. Newspapers, magazines, and books of all sorts contribute to the expansion of the mind. So can movies and TV shows. Through reading, we gain an understanding of concepts, ideas, theories, and basic information. Ours is a constantly changing world.

Advances in technology cause rapid changes. People lose their jobs. Thousands of people once made buggies. The automobile came and no more buggies. People must be prepared to learn new jobs. Ours is a constantly changing world. Reading is fundamental.

A Relaxing Vacation

[*Note:* This paragraph is especially incoherent and so needs extensive revision. In order to retain the information given yet to throw the focus on the title's premise (that we will be told in what way fishing is "relaxing"), you will have to subordinate, add sentences, and, perhaps, break the material into two paragraphs.]

Anyone who wants a relaxing vacation should try fishing. You need to know a lot to be successful at fishing. There are many books on the subject, and many of them are good. Boat safety is important to be aware of. People who fish need to know about boats. They need to know about tackle and rods. I recommend the Catskills area. I've often spent a whole day there without seeing anyone. On weekends it can be crowded and noisy. Yes, fishing can be a relaxing pastime.

6. Here are some topics ideal for comparison and/or contrast. Choose one, develop a thesis about it, and then write two paragraphs or clusters of paragraphs supporting your thesis, each proceeding in a different way. One should be organized point by point (A/B, A/B, A/B), the other in blocks (all

of A, then all of B). In each case provide the appropriate transitions and specify your mode of procedure (point by point or blocked).

Before and after Watergate

The American ideal, the American reality

The university, past and present

Two summers in my life

Two novels or two authors

My closest friends

High school and college

Football and baseball

Two TV shows or two movies

Liberal versus conservative

Romantic love and marriage

7. Rearrange and revise for coherence the sentences in each of the following groups, subordinating some and providing others with appropriate transitions. Each group should yield a tolerable paragraph once rewritten.

   a. (1) The time seemed right.
   (2) We had planned every detail of the trip.
   (3) We did not have as good a time as we had hoped.
   (4) We had every reason to be optimistic.
   (5) Nothing turned out as we had planned.
   (6) We decided to go.

   b. (1) Some people get good jobs without a degree.
   (2) All professionals have degrees.
   (3) Most such jobs go to college-educated men and women.
   (4) A college degree is a stepping-stone to a good job.
   (5) Most top corporate executives have degrees.
   (6) Going to college is a wise move indeed.
   (7) A college education is worthwhile in and of itself.

   c. (1) Money in the pipeline will be spent as appropriated.
   (2) No money will be available for any new project.
   (3) The committee met for three hours.

(4) No new programs have been proposed as of now.
(5) It's too early to say how the lack of funds will impact the staff.
(6) No decision was reached.

d. (1) The actors believed in the play.
(2) It closed only two weeks after it opened.
(3) The public didn't come.
(4) The critics gave it rave reviews.
(5) The playwright killed herself.
(6) The play closed.

8. In the following passages, underline all transitions and anything else that makes for coherence (for instance, the repetition of a word or the use of a pronoun) and then name the kind of organization that each exhibits.

a. Basically, there are two ways of organizing a comparison and/or a contrast. First, a comparison/contrast can be organized in what we might call "staccato" fashion: A/B, A/B, A/B. Then, the one or the other might proceed by way of blocks: first all of A and then all of B, with the comparison/contrast drawn in the B block. Of course, there are other ways of organizing a comparison/contrast. But the two I've just outlined are the basic ways, the ones that most often serve the writer's aims.

b. Why do we wear clothes? Well, obviously, clothes protect us from the elements. In winter, for instance, clothes help keep us warm, we creatures with no natural protection. No less important, clothes provide us with protection in the workplace: they protect a welder from sparks, a plumber from hot solder, a teacher from the grasping (and dirty) hands of schoolchildren. But by far the most important reason why we wear clothes is their symbolic value: through our clothes we express ourselves, tell who we are or at least want to be seen as being, signify our class and position in the world. Clothes, then, are necessary for utilitarian reasons. Even if we didn't have such reasons, however, we would still need clothes. For it is through them that we identify ourselves to each other and thus help order our social lives.

c. On our trip to Egypt this summer, we arrived at Cairo on Tuesday morning, June 22. After spending two days in Cairo, we went to Alexandria. Alexandria was disappointing, but thereafter our tour was nothing but wonderful. For instance, the tomb of Rameses II, which we saw on the sixth day, was thrilling. And the Valley of the Kings, where we spent the last two days of the tour, was incredible. On the flight home we had much to reminisce about.

d. There is much to see in Giza, which is on the outskirts of Cairo. First, of course, one is struck by the Great Pyramid of Cheops, the largest and most impressive of the pyramids. Behind and somewhat below the Cheops pyramid are two other pyramids, which form a truly impressive backdrop. Beyond all three and still further down the slope is the sphinx, the one that everyone has seen pictures of. About two hundred feet below the sphinx are a number of shops dealing in miniature sphinxes and other such tourist items. And not fifty feet below these shops is a ditch, which circles the entire site, meant to control the recent influx of water that is destroying the sphinx and even threatens the pyramids. Beyond this, the traveler will find refreshment stands, which are sorely needed given the incredibly hot Egyptian sun.

e. Of the two ways to determine the best shot for a photograph, I prefer the first way—simply eyeballing the subject matter and judging accordingly. To be sure, the other way—using a light and distance meter—will invariably produce a decent picture, whereas eyeballing will not. But a decent picture is not a great picture. Great pictures result not from instruments but from the sharp eye and the experience of a skilled photographer. All the instruments in the world cannot replace the educated eye behind the camera.

CHAPTER 4

Organization II:
Paragraph to Paper

All writing is divided into three parts. We've already looked at beginnings; middles and endings await. Because there's much more to say about middles than about endings, we'll defy logical order and take up endings first. Then we'll consider middles at length and conclude with whole papers: beginning, middle, and end.

ENDINGS

Like beginnings, endings are psychological in function. Also like beginnings, endings are particularly difficult, or at least many people find them so. The difficulty of ending is eased, however, if you remember what an ending should do: whereas the beginning should draw the reader in, the ending should wrap things up, tie everything together, and give the reader a sense of completion. That's why a single sentence telling the reader that the essay is finished would be no better in most cases than a single sentence at the beginning announcing the thesis. For the most part, a single sentence would simply not be satisfying. Furthermore, there should be no arguing at the end, just as there should be none at the beginning. Argument is the function of the middle.

Summarizing and Restating

What, then, can be done to bring things to a point and thus to impart a sense of closure? A summary is one possibility. The summary pulls ideas together and reminds the reader of the main points made in the essay, some of which the reader may have lost sight of. Especially when writing a longer paper, consider the summary as a possible way of ending. A full summary, however, is not generally as well suited to the short essay, for readers can be counted upon to retain the points through, say, five to ten paragraphs. But a brief summary of a sentence or two in combination with, perhaps, a concluding statement can serve the needs of any kind of paper. The two samples that follow, each the conclusion of a paper whose beginning is to be found on pages 31 and 32, respectively, exemplify this kind of ending.

> In sum, for a team to kill off a powerplay successfully, the players must forecheck aggressively, clear out the front of the net, and get good goal-tending from the goalie. In other words, winning takes a concerted effort from all the players on the ice. And the effort must be one to win, not just to intimidate the opposing team.
>
> EDWARD BENDERNAGEL

> Memory, language, and a sense of space or boundary are the vehicles that Muir uses to show that man and beast are worlds apart. While many human beings will always relate to animals in human terms, to do so is in fact both futile and silly, Muir suggests. The lecturing of pets on their failure to observe household rules, for instance, or to distinguish one room from another is not only pointless but downright absurd.
>
> SIU LAU

Look back and compare the sample beginnings with these sample endings. Note especially how each ending makes reference to each sample beginning. This referring back by restating the thesis or repeating a key phrase in the thesis paragraph helps to give an essay a sense of roundness—because the end rounds back to the beginning—and thus a satisfying sense of closure.

Analogy

Another possible way to end is with an analogy that both summarizes (albeit indirectly) the argument of an essay and widens its scope. Here, for instance, is the ending of a paper whose thesis is that "television can play a positive role in one's development" (page 31):

In a movie I remember seeing when I was little, a witch with a crystal ball could see anywhere in the world and anyone. She could summon up whatever person she had in mind and whatever place—past, present, or future. Her ability, of course, was deemed miraculous and magical. But, the future excepted (they're working on it, though), we each have that magic ball: we call it TV. Like the gypsy's crystal, TV shows us every day the whole panorama of present and past. If viewed with discrimination, therefore, television is truly a window on the world, and as such it can be a positive force in one's development.

Terence Mulgrew

Question and Answer

Another way to end is to ask a question about some central point raised in the middle of the essay and then answer it. This is the pattern of the following sample, the ending of a paper about a short story, set in a Nazi concentration camp, in which an adolescent named Stella regresses to infantile behavior and her mother, Rosa, goes mad at the end.

But why does Stella regress as she does? The answer the story points to is, clearly, her enforced condition of helplessness. With no control whatever over her life in the external world, she falls back upon the strategies of the infant for a fantasy sense of control. It might be noted that much the same is true of Rosa herself at the end of the story. Through Stella and, at the last, through Rosa, the story brings home with great force what it means to be a victim: it is to be a child with no possible place of refuge except one's own mind.

The Reverse Funnel

While moving from question to answer, this last sample also incorporates another way of ending (the ways we've looked at are not mutually exclusive), a way suitable to short and long papers alike: that is, moving from the particular to the general, from the specific supports of one's thesis to a statement that fans out to embrace a wide range of things and/or people. The statement must be related to one's thesis, of course, but it must also be of greater scope. Called the "reverse funnel," though "megaphone" might be more apt metaphorically, this kind of an ending can be used along with any other kind. It is especially satisfying because it links the concerns of an essay to the world at large and thus suggests the relevance of the essay's thesis to the reader's life. Note how the next ending, which makes reference to the governing thesis of the sample beginning on page 34, fans out to generalization and how that generalization provides a satisfactory sense of closure.

"The Road Not Taken," then, concerns the difficulty that choice entails for us: our reluctance to choose, our mixed feelings once we have chosen, and our tendency to rationalize our choices at some later date. We must choose, but making choices is difficult both because of the imponderables of the external world and especially because of the conflicts within. The irony of it is that, unlike most people who have lived on this earth, *we* have the luxury of choice but often find that luxury burdensome. Freedom of choice, it seems, brings its own set of problems and its own psychological dilemmas.

Two things should be noted about this paragraph. First, the next-to-last line—"unlike most people who have lived on this earth, *we* have the 'luxury of choice'"—refers back to the thesis paragraph via the word "luxury." Again, referring back like this helps give an essay a sense of roundness and thus closure. Second, while beginning with a quick summary, this sample ending attains final resolution through a generalized statement. Opening out to suggest wide applicability, this way of ending—the reverse funnel—readily gives an essay the effect of climax, the feel of closure, the sense of an ending.

One more word about endings: like beginnings, endings must be carefully worded. For instance, when writing an ending, choose some key words or phrases from the beginning of your paper. If you think carefully about your purpose, choosing them should be easy enough. Then be sure to put things in terms that your thesis and your own logic require, because a misstatement is particularly noticeable and particularly damaging at the end. Here is an instance of misstatement:

Television can teach us about and familiarize us with our world. To be sure, our education, families, and friends are undoubtedly the main influences that shape the people we become. However, practically every person in the United States watches television every day; therefore, television is very educational.

The last sentence, which should be the climax, of this ending does not deliver what it should. For one thing, it begs the question (just because people watch TV does not make it educational); moreover, it does not really follow from the sentences that precede. Consequently, the reader is left dangling, without a sense that things have been tied up, without a sense of an ending. Now compare this paragraph with the following, in which the last sentence is restated to fit the context:

Television can teach us about and familiarize us with our world. To be sure, our education, families, and friends are undoubtedly the main influences that shape the people we become. However, because practically every person in the United States watches television every day, it, too, must influence us in one way or another, and that influence should not be underestimated.

As restated, the paragraph now comes to a logical conclusion and a firm ending. It doesn't take much: just a few words dropped and added. But those few words make all the difference.

MIDDLES

Middle paragraphs contain the meat of any paper. Here is where the thesis is expanded upon, exemplified, argued, supported, or otherwise demonstrated. With the exception of paragraphs whose sole purpose is to provide transition, each middle paragraph must somehow develop an idea (as a rule, one per paragraph) that relates to the thesis and that helps explain why the writer believes and the reader should take seriously what the thesis states. The central or controlling idea of each middle paragraph is usually stated in a single sentence, generally called the "topic sentence" (or "sentences" if the statement takes, as is sometimes the case, two or even three sentences). The topic sentence may be found anywhere in a paragraph, but most commonly it comes at the beginning—the first sentence or the second if the first is transitional.

Internally, as we've seen, each middle paragraph must be organized according to an appropriate plan, like chronology or order of climax. In addition, like the sentences in a paragraph, the middle paragraphs of a paper must be arranged into some comprehensible sequence, with markers (transitions) all along the way. That is, just as one must decide what to put first, second, and so on within a paragraph, one must decide what sequence is best for the paragraphs themselves. Here, again, the ways of organizing we spoke of in Chapter 3 can come into play: should your thesis entail a list of steps, for instance, then enumeration could be your governing strategy, or enumeration along with order of climax, perhaps; or if your thesis involves a comparison/contrast, then that could provide your organizational pattern. In other words, everything you learned from Chapter 3 about organizing paragraphs internally applies equally to arranging the paragraphs within a paper. And so does what you learned about transitions. Just as transitions are often needed to relate sentences, they are often—indeed, usually—needed to relate paragraphs.

Having a suitable design in the first place and following through on it will provide a coherent foundation for any paper you write. But transitional links between middle paragraphs must be supplied when necessary, either at the end of one paragraph and/or the beginning of the next. Whenever a particular progression or relationship is not self-evident, even if the overall structure of the paper is clear, something to make the transition—that is, both to demarcate points and relate them—must be supplied. In the rewriting stage of every paper you do, be sure to check that the relationship of every paragraph, paragraph by paragraph, is clear and the movement fluid.

Keeping in mind what you have learned about middle paragraphs and transitions between them, study the sample essay that follows, noting how the paragraphs are linked (all transitions between paragraphs are underlined) and how that linkage makes the paper fluid and readable. (This, incidentally, is a transitional paragraph.)

Note: The first sample paper is on Frost's "The Road Not Taken," which you probably should review at this point—see Chapter 1. You will recognize the first and last paragraphs of the paper: they were used to exemplify the thesis paragraph and the reverse funnel ending.

The Problem of Choice

**Funnel
Beginning**

Thesis

Well over a hundred years ago, the British philosopher John Stuart Mill defined "modern" in connection with the freedom of choice: "[H]uman beings are no longer born to their place in life," Mill observed, "but are free to employ their faculties . . . to achieve the lot which may appear to them most desirable" (143). Our lives are no longer mapped out by tradition; we have the luxury of being able to choose what college to attend, whom we'll marry, what occupation we'll pursue. But upon what grounds can we make such choices? There's the rub. Our precious freedom leaves us in a quandary: we are often reluctant to choose and then ambivalent about the choices we've made. In "The Road Not Taken," Robert Frost dramatizes our difficulty by way of a speaker who is representative of us human beings loosed from the constraints of tradition but not fully comfortable with our relatively new freedom.

**Transition
Topic
Sentence**

Support

Before we turn to Frost's speaker, however, it should be noted that the situation described is symbolic, as most readers probably understand intuitively. Traveling down a road generally symbolizes life's journey, and a fork in the road signifies an important choice to be made as to the subsequent direction of one's life. This age-old symbolism is so common in our culture as to need no further comment. It should be remarked, though, that Frost uses these symbols with great skill: his treatment of them makes them seem fresh and newly meaningful.

**Transition
Topic
Sentences**

But to return to the poem's speaker, he expresses one reason for his difficulty in choosing his road at the beginning of the poem when he says, "sorry I could not travel both." That is, he didn't wish to make a choice at all. (His

Support

regret at having to choose, incidentally, is implied as well by the poem's title.) Confronted with an important choice, most of us feel the same; we would eat our cake and have it too. When asked what she might like to be, a child I know replied: "a policewoman, a reporter, a ballet dancer, and a doctor." Along the line, of course, she will narrow her list down, finally, to one occupation, but probably with a certain sense of narrowness and of lost possibilities.

Support

To some extent, we all regret not being able to take all of the roads before us. At any rate, the speaker's difficulty in choosing--as that difficulty stems from his wishing not to limit his possibilities--is internal, an aspect of the psychology of the chooser rather than inherent

Transition

in the things he must choose between.

Topic Sentence

But this second potential source of diffi-culty, a source external to the self, is sug-gested as well as the poem moves on. Though the

Support

speaker says that one of the two roads "was grassy and wanted wear," he immediately refutes himself by saying that in fact the two roads were exactly the same, equally worn and equally covered "In leaves no step had trodden black." So, really, there was no rational basis for a choice of road. This kind of difficulty is in-herent externally in the things that must be

Support

chosen between. The speaker's reaction to this external difficulty, however, takes us again to the inner sphere, and once again we see that the speaker's thought and feeling are marked by re-luctance and ambivalence--expressed now by the speaker's desire to keep the other road "for another day." With so little basis upon which to choose, what else could one feel? He feels what many of us feel, having little more basis for our choices than he had for his.

Transition

This lack of basis along with the feelings

Support

the lack produces helps explain the last stanza of Frost's poem. Here, the speaker takes us from the past (stanzas 1-3) to the distant future ("ages and ages hence"), suggesting thereby how for us the past remains present and always conditions the future. Sometime way in the future, he tells us, he will say that his reason for choosing the road that he did was that it was "the one less traveled by," the one that "was grassy and wanted wear." But we know that this will be a rationalization for a choice made regretfully and without any real basis. Yet who among us would say, "I chose my college, my ca-

Support

reer, my wife or husband by the flip of a coin"? Psychologically, we need to feel that we have chosen, even if--no, especially if--chance has been what in fact has directed us. And when enough time has gone by, we do start to remember reasons for choices that had no rational basis

Topic Sentence

in fact. Frost's speaker underscores this process by his projection into the future of his future distortion of the past.

Reverse Funnel Ending

"The Road Not Taken," <u>then,</u> concerns the difficulty that choice entails for us: our reluctance to choose, our mixed feelings once we have chosen, and our tendency to rationalize our choices at some later date. We must choose, but making choices is difficult both because of the imponderables of the external world and especially--as Frost drives home--because of the conflicts within. The irony of it is that, unlike most people who have lived on this earth, we have the luxury of choice but often find that luxury burdensome. Freedom of choice, it seems, brings its own set of problems and its own psychological dilemmas.

Major and Minor Supports

Middle paragraphs support the thesis of an essay. In analyzing how they do so, it is useful to see the topic sentence as supporting the thesis and everything else in a paragraph as supporting the topic sentence. Further, supporting material can be subdivided into major support and minor support. Minor support underpins major support, which in turn supports the topic sentence(s) of the paragraph. Most of the segments labeled *support* in the sample paper can be identified as major or minor. The third paragraph, which follows, provides a clear example:

Topic Sentences
> But to return to the poem's speaker, he expresses one reason for his difficulty in choosing his road at the beginning of the poem when he says, "sorry I could not travel both." That is, he didn't wish to make a choice at all. (His regret at having to choose, incidentally, is implied by the poem's title.)

Major Support
> Confronted with an important choice, most of us feel the same; we would eat our cake and have it too.

Minor Support
> When asked what she might like to be, a child I know replied: "a policewoman, a reporter, a ballet dancer, and a doctor." Along the line, of course, she will narrow her choice down, finally, to one occupation, but probably with a certain sense of narrowness and lost possibilities.

Minor Support
> To some extent, we all regret not being able to take all of the roads before us.

Major Support
> At any rate, the speaker's difficulty in choosing--as that difficulty stems from his wishing not to limit his possibilities--is internal, an aspect of the psychology of the chooser rather than inherent in the things he must choose between.

Here, the fifth and sixth sentences along with the seventh sentence offer minor support for the major support statement that "most of us feel the same," which itself expands upon the topic statement that the speaker "didn't wish to make a choice at all." The last sentence also provides major support for the paragraph's topic statement, which itself goes to back up the thesis statement that "Robert Frost dramatizes our difficulty" as to the making of choices.

Outlining

As we've seen, it is useful to think of middle paragraphs in terms of topic sentence(s), major support, and minor support. This is one of the ways in which outlining can be done.

You probably learned a good deal about outlining in high school, and, like most people (including me), you've probably forgotten most of it. I must confess that I never outline before I begin writing. For me, at least, outlining beforehand seems to impede the flow of ideas. If you do an outline first, however, fine. Some things work for some people and not for others. But maybe you can learn something from my practice.

I outline, after a fashion, not before but *after* I have a draft in hand—nothing elaborate, just a general support outline. That is, I quickly outline each paragraph as to topic sentence, major support, and minor support—as was just done with the third paragraph of the sample paper. In this way, I can see whether or not my paragraphs hold together and, if not, what needs to be done where. This type of outline also provides an easy way to check on coherence, for it shows where transitions are probably needed (between all major segments). Take the paragraph entitled "My Worst Course," found in the exercises at the end of the last chapter. The support outline that follows shows immediately what's wrong and what must be done. (For convenience, I have broken the paragraph into sentences.) The outline shows (by "??") what needs to be deleted or, if kept, restated. It shows as well where linkage is needed (at the points marked with a ^) and where firming up is needed so that the reader will clearly see what supports what.

Topic Sentence	The course I took last term in psychology was disappointing.
Major?	I'm interested in what makes people tick.
??	I love history.

Major	The course I had seemed to be only about rats.
Minor	We studied rats running mazes, rats going mad in deprivation chambers, rats getting electrocuted.
Major? Minor? ^	Rats hold a certain amount of interest.
Major? ^	Rats are not people.
??	As I said, I love history.
Major? ^	People are what I'm interested in.
Conclusion ^	My psych course was disappointing.

In the rewrite that follows, note how relationships have been clarified, as has what supports what.

Topic Sentence	The course I took last term in psychology was disappointing.
Major	It was so because I'm interested in what makes people tick.
Major	But the course I had seemed to be only about rats.
Minor	We studied rats running mazes, rats going mad in deprivation chambers, rats getting electrocuted.
Major	No doubt, rats hold a certain amount of interest; however, rats are not people.
Minor	And, as I said, people are what I'm interested in.
Conclusion	That's why my psych course was disappointing.

This kind of an outline could provide you with a check on your writing, too. If you can't outline each paragraph of your own more or less as I have outlined the rewritten paragraph here, then something needs to be attended to. A support outline will also provide a check on coherence by showing you where to supply transitions if needed. This kind of outlining may not be for you, but try it with your next first draft. You might find it as helpful as I do.

Paragraphing

For any kind of outline to work for you, of course, you must have a sense of what paragraphing itself is all about. By now, you probably do, but a quick review wouldn't hurt.

Any composition contains three kinds of paragraphs: beginning, middle, and ending. Beginnings and endings we're finished with; it's middle paragraphs that we're interested in at this point. The typical middle paragraph develops one idea, expressed in its topic sentence. Therefore, when you move from one idea to another, begin a new paragraph. Keep in mind, however, that middle paragraphs are not self-contained; they must relate to the thesis of the paper and also to one another.

The sample paper on "The Road Not Taken" found earlier in this chapter can once more serve as our model. Look back at it again and observe that each middle paragraph has one topic sentence, one controlling idea. Note, too, the average length of the paragraphs. An average paragraph, like most of the paragraphs in the sample, runs from a third to two-thirds of a typed page. You should judge your paragraphs against this norm. Granted, some will be shorter and some longer. The second paragraph of the sample paper, for instance, is a good deal shorter than the norm, for its idea doesn't need much development. And transitional paragraphs are generally short—two or three sentences or even just one. Short paragraphs can also be used for emphasis or special effect, as can exceptionally long paragraphs. But most paragraphs should fall within a range of five to twelve sentences. They should because it generally takes five to twelve sentences to develop an idea adequately. And that brings us to our next topic.

Paragraph Development

You've seen how to develop both a beginning and an ending. Now, how can middle paragraphs be developed? The answer is, in many ways. Here is a list of the most common. We'll look more closely at some of these in the following pages.

Cause and effect—exploring the causes or consequences of something

Description—portraying a person, place, or whatever with concrete details

Evaluation—giving reasons for a value judgment

Comparison/contrast—pointing up likenesses or differences between one thing and another

Classification—breaking something into its classes or types and then discussing each in turn

Exemplification—providing examples—for instance, with an anecdote

Definition—specifying the meaning of terms or concepts related to a thesis

Appeal to authority—backing up a statement by reference to experts, statistics, or the authority of one's own experience

Logical inference—drawing conclusions from the evidence presented

Analogy—drawing conclusions based on similarity

These methods or modes of development or procedure are not mutually exclusive. They may be used in combination; the topic of a given paragraph and your purpose will dictate the appropriate method or combination of methods.

An example at this point should be helpful. Here is a sample middle paragraph in which six different methods of development are used:

Topic Sentence	No words could capture the bleakness of the Dust Bowl in the Great Depression. We have never
Comparison	seen anything like it except, perhaps, the landscape we've come to know of the moon. It was totally barren, devoid of a single living crea-
Comparison **Example**	ture. Deserts are more alive. Not one stalk of corn grew in the five counties of Kansas that now form the buckle of the corn belt. As one
Authority	journalist wrote at the time, "The Dust Bowl is the greatest disaster of an age of disasters."

Description ⎤ Just try to picture it: light-brown dust every-
where--the color of the land, the color of the
air, the color of the sky. Nothing but grit to
see, to breathe, to taste with every waking
Cause and ⎱ minute. What could produce desolation on such a
Effect   ⎰ scale? Lack of irrigation was the cause. Once
the depression struck, farmers could not afford
to irrigate their land, which required irrigation to yield a crop. Cause and effect became a
vicious cycle once the cause--the lack of irri-
gation--took hold, for the lack of a crop put
the ability to irrigate still farther out of
reach. Thus, the land became barren, and, thus--
Statistics ⎱ as the Bureau of Statistics has estimated--five
million farm families had to take to the road.

Of course, most paragraphs don't incorporate as many methods of development as this one. Now let's focus on some selected methods and see how each can generate a paragraph by itself.

Exemplification. Exemplification is of special importance. Indeed, examples are the lifeblood of essays. Concrete instances are necessary to animate the abstractions of a thesis or topic sentence by showing how they relate to our everyday world, which we rightly take as our measuring rod. Note how the abstraction of the topic sentence of the following paragraph is made clear by the example (which here involves contrast).

There are many conflicts between what the Catholic Church teaches and the attitudes—upon which people act—of society at large. For example, my church teaches that one should be a virgin until marriage, that sex is appropriate only in marriage, and that marriage is for life. Marriage is a sacrament, a holy institution, and should be entered upon with great gravity. About such things, we have no choice; we must do as taught. In contrast, society holds that we must decide such matters for ourselves. Moreover, most people seem to think that virginity is something to be corrected as fast as possible, that marriage is nothing but a legal formality, and that the purpose of sex is merely pleasure, to be had as much and as often as possible. All you need do is to tune into TV or go to a few movies to see how different society's attitudes are from those of the church. How, then, can there be a reconciliation of the two? [The last sentence is a transition to the next paragraph.]

SCOTT DINNELL

Definition. Definitions usually incorporate examples, as do, for instance, most definitions in a dictionary. The next paragraph, from a paper on the meaning of liberty, proceeds by definition (along with examples).

But what is freedom? Does freedom mean that anyone can do anything that he or she likes? No, that's not freedom; that's anarchy. Or is freedom "just another word for nothing left to lose," as Janis Joplin put it? If so, then not only are most people not free but the American ideal of "the pursuit of happiness" is a sham. At least it is a sham if we view happiness, as most of us do, as tied to "having"—not just things, but relationships, children, intellectual attainments. However different, these definitions share something fundamental, something that invalidates both equally: they both define freedom in such a way as to make it external to the self. In contrast, my definition of freedom is internal: freedom is the ability to act appropriately in the present. To take a negative instance, how many men respond to their wives or wives to their husbands as though they were their mothers or fathers? We keep reliving the past and so do not live in the present. Laying down the baggage of the past and living now, in the present—that is what freedom is. Freedom, then, is psychological, a state of being having nothing to do with externals.

JOANNE DE LA CRUZ

Appeal to Authority. Appeal to authority is the developing and supporting of a point by quoting, paraphrasing, or summarizing experts in a field or, simply, by referring to one's own experience. The following paragraph incorporates both kinds of appeal.

People seem always in such a rush, chasing from appointment to appointment, from party to party, never allowing themselves the peaceful moments that come in self-reflection when one is alone. As for me, I agree with Thoreau:

I love to be alone. I never found the companion that was so companionable as solitude. We are for the most part more lonely when we go abroad among men than when we stay in our chambers.

How true that last sentence is! At a party I went to last year, for instance, only three or four people knew each other. Everyone else just stood around looking stupid. I felt terribly alone, as I'm sure everyone else did except those few I mentioned. In contrast, I never feel alone at home in my chair reading. My thoughts provide all the company I need.

JUDY CARIFTO

Analogy. Analogy is a type of inference based on the assumption that if things are alike in some significant way, they are probably alike in other ways as well. An analogy is not proof, but it is often an effective way of clarifying. Here is a clear example involving an analogy between gun-control laws and Prohibition.

Gun-control laws don't work. Thousands of them already clutter the books of local and state governments, yet no one has found that these laws have prevented even one crime. It is indeed, however trite, the person and not the gun who commits a crime. But we Americans, who made alcohol illegal for a decade (I'm speaking of Prohibition), should know better. What was the effect of Prohibition? It was to create—and that's exactly the right word—organized crime in America. Why? Because people would not obey such a silly law. It was the law itself, then, that fostered crime. So, too, gun-control laws: they will only take guns out of the hands of the innocent citizen and put them solely into the hands of the criminal. In a word, gun laws will be about as effective as Prohibition. They will do little but foster organized crime.

THOMAS NOVAK

ARRANGING MIDDLE PARAGRAPHS

In the last chapter we discussed ways of organizing middle paragraphs and, in this chapter, ways of developing them. One question remains: how can middle paragraphs best be arranged to satisfy the reader and achieve the writer's purpose? There is no single answer. Given the infinite variety of subjects and purposes for writing, there must be many ways of organizing essays. And indeed there are. Some, however, are so common and so adaptable to many situations that they are worth careful study. They are, as you might have guessed, chronology, spatial sequence, comparison and contrast, enumeration, and order of climax. We have already seen these structures in Chapter 3, as ways of organizing paragraphs. Now we shall focus on them as ways of determining the most effective arrangement of paragraphs in the paper. Six student papers follow, with certain crucial transitions printed in italics to clarify how the paragraphs are arranged. The first five papers exemplify the five basic kinds of paper structure. The sixth exemplifies another kind of structure and is included to suggest that there are other ways of organizing papers, though the five basic ways remain basic. If you master these, they will serve you well. Then you can strike out on your own.

Chronology

Memories of Me

Ever since I was a little girl, I have saved various memorabilia touching my life—everything from kindergarten doodles to Yankee ticket stubs. *Organized chronologically*, all of these items can be found in three albums, which together hold the story of my life.

My *first* album contains photographs, drawings, and writings from my *early childhood* to my *graduation from grammar school*. First there are pictures of me as a baby; then come my early attempts at writing my own name, one in purple crayon, one in bright green, one in pink. Next there is a picture of me at age six with a broken leg. And then the report cards start. Finally, after a collection of pictures of me in my tomboy phase—of me playing baseball with the boys, for instance—come my last report card and pictures of my graduation from grade school.

My *last* album is not yet complete. It moves *from my freshman year* in college to *the present, the beginning of my senior year*. Opening it up, I find materials from orientation, which was held the week before the first classes, my first freshman papers (ugh!), and my freshman beanie, with propeller. Then, there I am with my boyfriend after we had just met—at the beginning of my sopho-more year—followed by articles I wrote for the school paper and copies of the dean's list from each term of my junior year. For the album to be complete, all that is needed now are pictures of my college prom and graduation.

Well, *time moves on*, and very quickly for the most part. My third album will soon be complete and this part of my life will soon be over. And once it is? I have bought a fourth album, and it's just waiting to be filled.

LAURA LALAINA

Spatial Sequence

Self-Expression

We express ourselves in many ways. In fact, just about every-thing we do tells something about us—the clothes we choose, the foods we prefer, and on and on. But most of all, perhaps, we reveal who we are by what we surround ourselves with. To know a person's home is to know the person.

Take me, for example, or my home. Let me take you for a tour around my *place* to show what I mean. We'll start in the *basement*, where you would get—if you were really there—a demonstration of my trains. I have wonderful trains—Lionel O gauge in mint condition. And my layout is terrific. Notice the two mountain routes and the three interlinked valley routes. The system takes four transformers to run and has twenty switching tracks. It really is something, and I love it. I've been collecting trains and building my layout for twelve years now.

Climbing the cellar stairs and turning right, we come to the family room. My parents let me do as I like here, so what you see tells you about me. First, there is my collection of over two hun-dred records, from classical, to jazz, to rock. Notice, also, the double bass, which I've studied for the last seven years, and the music—from Bach to Basie.

Now, *one more flight of stairs and we're at* my room. There, there's a desk with a computer on it, a guitar on the bed, books in a bookcase, and a baseball bat in the corner. There are also Bruce Springsteen posters on the walls and a pile of dirty clothes on the floor. The room is not a mess, but then again it isn't exactly neat either. The wallpaper, which I helped pick out, is a bright Scottish plaid, and the curtains and bedspread are light red.

So, what have you concluded about me? I think I know. You see me as a hobbyist with, perhaps, a touch of the child in him; someone of varied interests and fairly broad tastes; a student, and probably a decent one; a person who is more or less easygoing but who has a few bad habits; and, on balance, someone who is basically cheerful and glad to be alive. You're right on all scores. I think I know myself pretty well, and now you know me, too. As I said, to know a person's home is to know the person.

CIARAN McKEEVER

Comparison and Contrast

A Matter of Face

There are many kinds of normal facial expressions. By "normal" I mean the expression a person normally goes about with, the expression a person comes to be associated with, as opposed to some momentary expression of happiness or grief. Momentary expressions only tell of what a person is feeling at that moment. A person's normal facial expression, however, can tell a great deal about that person generally.

For instance, take my two aunts, Aunt Marilyn and Aunt Eunice. The normal facial expression of each totally reveals the kind of person each is. Aunt Marilyn's normal expression is bright and cheery. Just looking at her face usually is enough to make me feel glad. And Aunt Marilyn's normal expression does indeed show the person within. She is, that is, a very bright and cheery person. Her bubbly love of life shines through her brilliant blue eyes; her warmth and openness show themselves in her broad smile. She never yelled at me when I was young, even if I was being mischievous. She would just grace me with one of her generous smiles and tell me to be more careful next time.

In utter contrast, my Aunt Eunice both has and is a sour puss. Her constricted personality announces itself in her beady little eyes. She characteristically squints, as though she is scrutinizing and judging everything and everybody she looks at. And she is!

Her habitually pursed lips reflect her dour personality. One little mistake on my part when I was young—a spilled glass of milk, an extra cookie sneaked—was all it took for her to turn into an avenging angel, or persecuting devil.

I've used the present tense here because what I've said of my aunts is as true today as when I was a child. In fact, as my aunts have aged, *the contrast between them seems greater than ever.* Aunt Marilyn is still bright and cheery, and, though older, she seems prettier than ever. She bakes me cookies and slips me an occasional ten dollars to help me keep my head above water at school. *Once more in contrast,* Aunt Eunice, whom I rarely see anymore, looks much uglier even than she did years ago. Her eyes are even beadier and her mouth is even more pursed, as if the sour grapes she used to seem to be tasting have turned into salted lemons. At any rate, what people are can often be seen in their normal facial expressions. Mine, I pray, is like Aunt Marilyn's and not Aunt Eunice's.

Tracy Masucci

Enumeration

My Summer Job

This summer, I had the good fortune of getting the opportunity to taste high-class living—or so I thought at the outset. I was hired as a waitress at a ritzy "members only" club on Long Island. Thinking that I would somehow acquire millions by, for instance, helping an old dowager and consequently being left her estate, or simply by marrying a member of the club, I walked into this job with a dazzling smile. However, my fantasy was cut short, for I soon realized that working for the rich brings no benefits at all, much less fringe benefits.

To begin with, the salary was terrible—five dollars an hour for bowing to bitches. As for tips, forget it! I soon found that the rich don't tip—for aren't tips taken care of by the members' dues? Dues or no dues, I got nothing from those greedy bastards, except of course, for insults and complaints about my service.

In the second place, I knew that I had turned sour, and I didn't like myself like that. Disenchanted with millionaires, I struggled not to pour coffee into the laps of my assigned members. These members, *my* members, sat and ate at my tables day after day. I knew them by name, by dish, by perfume or after-shave. In gratitude, they begged my attention by yelling, "Hey, Missy!" I would then trot over to their thrones like an obedient dog. I didn't like having turned sour, but I liked being an obedient dog (the cause) even less. The only enjoyment I had from this fiasco was dancing on bagel rounds in the kitchen, then tucking the chips into baskets and placing them on my "favorite" member's table.

And *finally*, there's my *last and greatest* grievance, the memories of my otherwise decrepit members.

Like elephants, they remembered everything, every spill, every slip-up. One woman even had the gall to remind me of a saltshaker I overturned on my very first day working at the club. And what do you think her husband was doing as she engaged in this bit of nostalgia? "Hubby" was sneaking a squeeze of my newly chubby behind (food was our real pay). I had to quit this job for my sanity, not to mention my figure. Now the new semester has begun. I never thought I'd say it, but it's nice to be back at school.

CLAIRE McMAHON

Order of Climax

The Air, the Water, the Waste

What a wonderful planet we live on, this blue and green place we call Earth! There is water enough for all and more than enough food, if we distributed it equitably. The sun cheers us, the air embraces us, and everywhere we are greeted by nature's beauty. Yet we are not thankful for these blessings. In fact, we seem to do everything we can to destroy the origin of our bounty with our waste. We are turning this beautiful world into a wasteland.

Just think, for instance, of what we're doing to the trees with acid rain. There is hardly a forest left in the Northern Hemisphere that does not show significant damage from this kind of air pollution. And many forests—like the Black Forest in Germany—have experienced a dieback of as much as a third of their growth. If nothing is done, the beauty of these preserves will be gone forever. And what will we do, one must ask, when the oxygen-supplying trees die off? It's not just beauty that is at stake.

In this light, the destruction of the rain forests in South America is *even more terrible*. It is estimated that these forests supply nearly 40 percent of the earth's oxygen. Yet they are being cut down at such a rate that all will be gone early in the next century. And for what? The land freed by their destruction is thin in topsoil and can produce food only for a few years, whereas the runoff from the cleared land will muddy and clog neighboring rivers for decades to come.

Equally terrible is what we seem to have done to the ozone layer, which protects us from the sun's harmful (ultraviolet) rays. It's now thought that some of our gaseous wastes, like Freon (wastes that combine with ozone) have created a hole in the ozone layer above each pole. It doesn't seem too much of a speculation to say that if we go on as we have been going, more holes will appear, but these over New York, Paris, and Moscow.

Worst of all, at least with regard to the near future, is what is happening to our rivers, streams, and underground aquifers. In both hemispheres, many streams and rivers have become clogged from runoff caused by our modes of agriculture. And more and more, we're finding that we have poisoned our aquifers with our waste—chemicals from industry, runoff from landfills, and so forth. We have even managed to pollute the oceans!

No, we have not been thankful for the bounty of the earth. Just the reverse—we have taken our planet for granted and given nothing back for all we have received. We must change our ways. If we don't, we will wake up one morning with only poison to drink; we won't be able to go outside because of the deadly rays; and, should we somehow survive these catastrophes, we all will ultimately suffocate from lack of oxygen. We have befouled our own nest. It's imperative that we now start cleaning it up.

AHN JI-HOON

Dialectical Structure

The next essay, while generally following a chronological pattern, also moves dialectically, from statement to counterstatement to a synthesis or balancing (in paragraph 3) of statement (paragraph 1) and counter-statement (paragraph 2). This is an elegant structure, though usable only with certain types of subject matter. I include the essay mainly to demonstrate that there are ways of structuring other than the five basic ways we've considered. Once you've mastered those, you might go on to try out a structure such as this.

Dialectical Spirituality

In childhood, we have little choice but to believe what we're told, especially in matters of religion. For us Catholics, the idea of God as Father—that is, as male—is ingrained as soon as we can lisp and make the sign of the cross. Impressed upon even the smallest of children is the maleness of the power that controls the universe—the sun, the moon, and the dear green earth. And the language of the Church has a distinctly male bias. For instance, I remember being assured that one day I would be "a soldier of Christ." To be sure, this emphasis on God as Father, as male, is tempered somewhat by the Virgin Mary, who, though less important, still merits two important prayers. Saints and martyrs, too, can be female. But I was drawn to male power; so it was the spectacular though rather cloudy picture of St. Sebastian in the *Lives of the Saints* that haunted my imagination and not that of the Little Flower quietly hemorrhaging to death. I was no young feminist, however, seeking power for myself. I idolized my God as I idolized my father. The strength and pain I was made to see in Christ through my mother's vivid description of the crucifixion caused love and pity to well up in me. I trusted in the love and redeeming power of God as I trusted in the strength and protective power of my father.

In my teenage years, my faith in God as well as in my father diminished, though faith still remained, albeit somewhat changed. The earth, eternally rolling in its appointed course, took all my imagination. My falling away from many of the religious conceptions of my childhood stemmed, I think, from a desire to know God in a tangible way. I started to feel God in nature—in storms, in the roll of the oceans, in all of the energy of the world. The hope of resurrection subtly modulated into a sense of the regeneration of all things in nature, the cycle of birth and decay ever renewing the greening of the world. The regeneration that I could witness all around gave me a sense of sustenance that rote prayer never had. I never felt alone in the presence of clouds, falling snow, or the green leaf-tips of early spring. Prayer was then the awareness of all of nature around me, stretching, winding, curving, growing. I was part of nature, too, a young thing growing into her own.

But now, this second phase of my spirituality seems incomplete, for it now seems to lack the human presence and humanity of my childhood Redeemer. Yet I cannot return to the religion of my childhood, with all its fears and superstitions. What I need, I now see, is a sense of Christ *in this world*, of nature imbued with His presence. I need to feel God as Christ in all of the humanity of His life on this earth. Even thinking this thought makes Him seem nearer. I feel both the sanctity of creation and the presence of the Creator.

MaryAnn McCarra

REVISING A GOOD PAPER

We've examined at some length the revision of incoherent work and looked at revised paragraphs and a whole paper—"The Jaspers" (page 39)—for unity and coherence. But what about revising a basically sound paper, of making the good better? In this regard, consider one more paper. The original draft is good; the revision is better. In contrasting the two, pay special attention to point and focus. The original tends to become blurred, or to go out of focus and so to muddy whatever point is being made. The revision clears up the problem mainly by way of cuts. When it comes to writing, less is usually more. The good can usually be made better by cutting out anything that is not central to the purpose. (The main things cut from the original essay are in italics. As you read the revision, note the effect of these cuts as well as of the polishing—a better word here, a more arresting phrase there—that has been done.)

Organizational Cultures: A Contrast

For the past two and one-half years, I have been a part-time bank teller. *However, not all of this time was spent at the same bank.*

For two years I was employed at Yorkville Federal Savings and Loan. *But recently I left there to work* at American Savings Bank. Why did I leave one bank to do the exact same job at another? Not money, for the salaries are comparable. The answer is that I could no longer tolerate the culture that is practiced at YFSL.

Culture, in general, is a difficult word to define, for it has multiple meanings. Therefore, I shall focus on "organizational culture." *Management* (9th ed.), by H. Koontz and H. Weihrich, defines organizational culture as "the general pattern of behavior, shared beliefs, and values that members of an organization have in common." Furthermore, organizational culture can be divided into weak cultures and strong cultures. *I have been employed in two banks, each of which has a different organizational culture.*

From 1988 to 1990 I was an employee of YFSL—*an organization that* has a weak culture. At first, I was a very slow worker because I was not comfortable with my new job. But I noticed that the experienced tellers were slow, too. After a few months, I was a speed demon on the banking computer, but the others still moved at their own slow pace. Jokingly, I made a comment to a teller about her speed. She shot back, "Listen, I'm not moving faster for anyone. I get the same pay whether I work fast or slow!" I did not follow her lead. I felt it was foolish to hold up the line, so I worked faster.

The two assistant managers, Liz Smith and Marge Mehr, *saw that I worked fast and so they liked me. I, in turn, liked them back. However, after about a year or so, I realized that they were* the worst of the bunch. Many customers *who came to my window* complained to me about them. The customers would say things like: "*That one over there, Ms. Smith, is such a witch!*" "Liz Smith must still be on her coffee break." "*Why doesn't Marge Mehr ever smile?*" At first, I defended my bosses, but not for long. The customers were so right about them.

Marge and Liz both had the attitude that "Yes, I am boss here, so I can take an hour break when I want to, *and these customers are damned lucky to be served by me!*" They practiced exactly what they subconsciously preached.

For example, the standard break time is fifteen minutes, but they would stay in the lounge and gossip—usually about the customers or us tellers—anywhere from forty-five minutes to an hour. The tellers needed them, but they didn't care. Often a signature had to be verified so I would go to them. Were they cooperative and understanding? HELL NO! Marge—the ultimate bitch—would shout, "Can't you see that I'm on my break? Don't bother me!" Eventually, they came to dislike me. One day in November of last year my mouth got me in trouble. After Liz had finished her usual hour break, I said, "Hey, Liz, Happy New Year."

I rang in the new year by finding another job. *I was not fired; I just couldn't tolerate that weak culture anymore. I wanted to work in a friendly place where there is a good working atmosphere and employees are treated with respect.*

I found such a place at American Savings Bank—where I have been employed since the beginning of the year. I like my job here even though the work is exactly the same as at YFSL. Technically, a bank is a bank wherever you go. *Deposits and withdrawals into and out of various accounts are made at all banks; similarly, all banks sell travelers checks and savings bonds; and all have long lines of customers. Nevertheless,* there is an immense difference between ASB and YFSL.

Unlike at my old job, I like everyone here at ASB very much. Now I work in a family-like atmosphere and, although I've been an employee for less than one year, the managers have already adopted me as one of their "kids." My managers—Frank Olds, Allison Nigel, and Susan Wrobel—are *wonderful people.* They are totally professional and strict bosses when the bank is busy, but are *my friends* when it isn't. *They are always present to help the tellers and they never take breaks when the bank is busy.* Customers also like them. *My managers treat every customer with respect—even the most annoying ones. My superiors seek to please all customers at all times. Their friendly smiles and warm dispositions pay off, for I hear that at Christmas time the lounge is filled with candy and home-baked goodies that the customers bring by way of saying "Thank you for such good service."*

I enjoy working for an institution with a reputation like that of ASB. Since banks are institutions geared to serving the public, a competent staff—like the one at American—is crucial. A staff that works well together and whose members have respect for each other will also respect the customers they must serve and so will serve them well. This type of staff is fostered in an organization that has a strong culture—a culture that stresses the importance of working as a team. In contrast, a weak culture fosters an "all-for-me" attitude. I've sampled a little of each and made my choice. Which culture would you want to be a member of?

Revision

For the past two and one-half years, I have been a part-time teller. For the first two years I was employed at Yorkville Federal Savings and Loan; for the past six months I have been at The American Savings Bank. Why did I leave Yorkville to do the exact same job at American Savings? Not money, for the salaries are comparable. What then? The answer is that I could no longer stand the culture of Yorkville Savings. I changed jobs in order to change organizational cultures.

As defined by H. Koontz and H. Weihrich in *Management* (9th ed.), *organizational culture* is "the general pattern of behavior, beliefs, and values that members of an organization have in common" (57). Further, Koontz and Weihrich hold that there are two types of organizational culture: weak and strong (62).

YFSL has a weak culture, which I came to understand a few months after I started on the job. I was slow at first because I didn't know the routine or how to work the computer, so I didn't notice that the experienced tellers moved little faster than I. After a few months, however, I became a speed demon on the computer, but the other tellers still moved at the same slow pace. Jokingly, I made a comment to the teller next to me about her speed. She shot back, "Listen, I'm not killing myself for anyone. I get the same pay whether I work fast or slow. Let the customers wait!"

The assistant managers, Liz Smith and Marge Mehr, were no better. Many customers voiced complaints about them, saying things like: "Those two are as slow as molasses." "Ms. Smith must *still* be on her coffee break." "Smith and Mehr must hold a record for goldbricking." At first I defended my bosses, but then I realized that the customers were right. Whether consciously or subconsciously, Marge and Liz felt that, since they were the bosses, they could take long breaks whenever they wanted to. They preached speed, but their practice belied their preaching. And it was their practice that most of the tellers took to heart.

Unable to tolerate this "weak" culture any longer, I rang in the new year by getting another job. Although you may think that a bank is a bank is a bank, and although what I do at American Savings is exactly what I did at YFSL, the difference in organizational culture between the two is dramatic. At ASB the tellers' motto is "Work fast and get the customers out promptly." And the assistant managers—Frank Olds, Allison Nigel, and Susan Wrobel—are nothing less than paragons of efficiency. All three are fully professional and, though warm and friendly, strict bosses when the bank is busy. I've not heard a single customer complain about them or about the service of the tellers under them. Consequently, the atmosphere at ASB is upbeat and positive.

In sum, my experience highlights the two types of organizational culture, weak and strong. A weak culture is marked by an every-man-for-himself attitude. A weak culture sponsors the feeling that one should get away with as much as possible, or that one should not do any more than the minimum amount of work. In consequence, customers are dissatisfied and a negative atmosphere prevails. A strong culture, on the other hand, promotes camaraderie and a sense of pulling together to get a job done. A strong culture focuses on achievement and reinforces one's sense of self-worth when one works well. Most important, a strong culture fosters a positive atmosphere, making work a pleasure and so inspiring people to do their best. Both types of culture, then, feed on themselves: a weak culture creates a negative atmosphere, causing employees to work slowly, at a minimum level, which only increases the negativity; a strong culture creates a positive atmosphere, causing employees to do their best and thereby engendering a sense of pride and so further accentuating the positive. Though a weak culture requires less effort, it is far less rewarding in terms of job satisfaction than a strong culture. I don't know about you, but I would rather work hard and feel satisfied than shirk and watch the clock all day waiting for quitting time.

LAURA LALAINA

EXERCISES

1. Outline each of the following middle paragraphs as to major and minor support. (You may wish to review pages 75–76.) One of the three is incoherent. Use your outline to spot what needs to be done to the paragraph and then rewrite it accordingly.

a. For these reasons I believe that the United States should not drop out of the United Nations. Further, I think that the United States should pay what it owes and if anything step up its level of funding. After all, despite all of our economic problems, we remain the richest country in the world. It is simply untrue, therefore, that we can't afford to give more. We can if we get our priorities straight. Indeed, we can afford to increase our support, and we should. Why should we? We should because of the hundreds of millions of sick and starving people around the world. Whatever else the United Nations does—including things that seem unfriendly to us—it has proven itself the best agency in the world for aiding sick and malnourished people. For instance, the United Nations is responsible for the eradication of smallpox—what an accomplishment that is!—and has fed more people than all other philanthropic agencies put together. But let us look more closely at statistics bearing on these statements.

b. So characters in fairy tales generally embody aspects of our psychology and psychological growth. Sleeping Beauty is a classic example. Pricked at sixteen, there she lies for a hundred years waiting to be kissed. Surely we have here an image of female sexuality, dormant and then, at the right time, aroused. "Sleeping Beauty" is more than a fantasy; it is a tale that reveals something about the psychosexual development of the female. "Snow White," "Rapunzel," and many other tales about girls hidden away until the time is ripe touch on the same theme. In each, a wicked stepmother or witch is the immediate cause of the maiden's removal; but symbolically, stepmother or witch represents an inner force (Freud called it the "super-ego") keeping the girl hidden until she is sexually mature. And it's not only fairy tales about girls that are psychologically symbolic. Many a tale of a boy falls into the same kind of pattern.

c. The United States should enforce harsh punishments for everyone caught with illegal drugs. Many celebrities take drugs. Indeed, just the other day there was a raid in Santa Barbara and seven movie stars were arrested. Judges often only fine celebrities, which is to give them nothing more than a slap on the wrist. When people see celebrities getting away with drug abuse, they feel, "If they can do it, why can't I?" We must make an example out of celebrities, thereby showing that anyone who uses drugs will go to jail.

2. Divide the following essay into *four* paragraphs. Be ready to state your reasons for your paragraphing.

Types of Men

Given how many men there are, there must be many different types. But I want to talk about just two, the two types I find most amusing: I call them the "necessatarians" and the "mamarians." The former feel that their presence is necessary for the existence of the world. If they were not here, the world would stop revolving or maybe explode. These men find it impossible to walk in front of a mirror, a window, or anything that shows their reflection without pausing to admire what they see. They usually drive sports cars, wear designer clothes, and feel that women should be honored by their presence. Any woman who is foolish enough to marry one of these men can look forward to a life of mirrors—in every room, even in the garage, and, of course, above the bed. The mamarians are men eternally devoted to their mothers. So they marry women as much like their mothers as they can find. And they expect their wives to act like their mothers and get them a full breakfast every morning, pick up the dirty clothes they drop anywhere, clean the house, do the washing, and so on, even if they (the wives) have careers of their own. If you marry one of these men, be prepared, too, to spend most evenings and all holidays with your mother-in-law, who will teach you everything from how to prepare her son's meatloaf to what kind of toilet paper to buy. She'll also come to your house to render further assistance and generously show you what you have been doing wrong. There's one thing especially to be said for this kind of a man: if he isn't at home or at work, you can rest assured that he's at his mother's. It has been my luck to have gone out with many men of both types. In fact, though I'm sure there are other types, I haven't gone out with any. Well, the way I look at it is, though they're not good for a relationship, at least they're good for a laugh!

Sandra Calvi

3.   Here is a series of paragraph endings and beginnings (that is, the ending of one paragraph and the beginning of the next) taken from this book but with transitions deleted from most. Decide where transitions between paragraphs are needed and supply them.

    a. With some thought of a possible way of organizing in mind, then, I begin to write.
       I have a firm idea—or thesis—in mind.

b. Indeed, in comparing my dog to my boyfriend, I often think that a dog is a better companion than a man.

A dog can't talk. Consequently, it can't scream or ask questions.

c. Needless to say, this was not the most enjoyable game I've ever been to, even if our seats were on the fifty-yard line.

John and I searched the parking lot for over two hours before finding our car.

d. The best place for a thesis statement is at the end of the first paragraph or paragraph cluster.

The reason a thesis statement should usually . . . come toward the beginning is quite simple: the reader needs to know what is being argued.

e. When a writer fails to consider the intended audience, then communication most likely will not take place.

Judging an audience and writing with it in mind are not burdensome tasks.

Now go through the text of the present chapter and decide how its paragraphs are linked. If they are linked by transitions, jot down what the transitions are. If they are related in some other way, note what that way is in each case. Label your answers with page and paragraph numbers thus: p. 66, par. 1–2, par. 2–3; pp. 67, par. 4 to p. 68, par. 1; p. 68, par. 1–2, 2–3.

4. Here are some sentences, each of which could be a topic sentence of a middle paragraph. Decide how each could best be developed into a middle paragraph. Label each accordingly. (The list of ways of development is found on pages 78–79.)

a. However, the school will go under if nothing is done.

b. But no one could say that my uncle didn't really love his children.

c. This only goes to show that few people understand what manic-depression is.

d. It shouldn't be surprising, then, when I say that my wife sometimes reminds me of Wonder Woman.

e. The question still remains as to exactly what happened when the factory exploded.

f. Especially because of these likenesses, it's amazing how different I am from my brother.

g. In order to understand why America moved in such a direction, we must listen to what our greatest nineteenth-century writers said about the matter.

h. Granted, then, that all was lost, we must inquire into what could bring about so dire a result.

i. Mr. Williams also had the most interesting face I think I've ever seen.

j. In other words, the first thing you will need to know is how the engine works.

k. What must be concluded from all of this is self-evident.

l. Nevertheless, the book is well worth reading.

5. Here are six theses, any one of which could form the basis of a paper. Study them and decide what kind of overall organization (that is, of the whole hypothetical paper in each case) would be best suited to each thesis statement (chronology, enumeration, and so forth).

a. Over the course of the last thousand years, the image of Christ has changed in Western art.

b. There are several kinds of map, each suited to a different purpose.

c. As Eisenhower walked out of the White House and Kennedy walked in, we realized that we had begun a new era.

d. In its first century, America was idealistic; in its second, it was materialistic; and now it seems a bit of both.

e. Freud thought of the mind as a place divided into three regions: ego, superego, and id.

f. We shall examine the economic situation closely, moving from the least significant causes of our present difficulties to the most.

6. Revise the following paper by cutting out whatever is unnecessary and so causes it to lose focus and thus point; by providing transitions within paragraphs and between them as necessary; and by restating anything that seems muddy. Also, give the paper a reverse funnel ending.

Entertaining a Child

Entertaining a child can be a difficult task. Parents spend hundreds of dollars on toys only to find their children bored after ten minutes. Having babysat my brother, I have discovered many games that will entertain any child for hours.

This first game I call "I've got your nose." This game is played by placing the thumb between the middle and index fingers and then pulling on the child's nose. I then tell my brother that I have his nose in my hand. He's such a good kid. I really love him. He's so easy to get along with. And he's so easy to take in. He spends twenty minutes trying to devise a plan to get back his nose. He loves to plan sneak attacks on me to get his nose back. When he feels desperate, he pretends to have my nose and offers to make a trade. By the time I give his nose back, we've played for more than an hour.

We play a game I call "Why are you hitting yourself?" I take Teddy's arms and lightly hit him in the face with his own hands. Teddy is his name. I love that name, because he is a little Teddy Bear. I then repeat "Why are you hitting yourself?" approximately a hundred times. He struggles to overpower me, but of course I'm too strong for him. He may not admit that he loves the game, but he does. His squeals of laughter fill the room every time we play it. The laughter of kids is the best. I love to hear kids laugh. I think it's a show.

The third game we play I call "The lazy man's hide-and-seek." My brother hides while I sit on the couch. I then call out places he might be. "Are you in the bathroom?" I ask. "No," he answers. "The closet?" "No." "The kitchen?" "Aw, you found me." Teddy will then come out laughing and proceed to find a different hiding place. My favorite part of this game is that, while he is hiding, I get to watch TV and see some of my favorite shows. I like reruns of "Lucy" especially, and some of the soaps.

I entertain Teddy for hours with these games. He doesn't need toys, just attention.

Terence Mulgrew

CHAPTER 5

Other Aspects of Expository Writing

After you've mastered everything we've covered in the last four chapters, you should be able to write readable prose. For, having mastered that material, you now know how to present a thesis and to develop it coherently—and that's what makes writing readable. However, the best writing involves more than mere readability. Effective prose, prose that a reader remembers and is swayed by, is not only readable but also interesting and enjoyable. This and the next chapter will show you how writers create interest and enjoyment. You should experiment for yourself with these various ways of making writing interesting, not all at once, but one per paper, perhaps, for the next ten to fifteen papers you write. Master each separately; then all will be available to you in the future.

NARRATION

An essay can be entirely narrative. Stories of people doing things as they move through time—including biographical, autobiographical, and historical essays—are all narratives. A typical historical essay on the Watergate fiasco, for instance, might proceed to tell the story of how the break-in came about and its aftermath, moving chronologically from the beginning of the affair to the end. Biographical essays proceed in exactly the same manner. Autobiographical essays also usually move chronologically. The following essay provides an excellent example of a narrative essay that is chiefly autobiographical.

So Much for Philosophy!

This past weekend I had the immeasurable pleasure of dining with Benito and Rose Bisogno, two friends of my parents from the "old country," as they frequently call Italy. This delightful ritual takes place once a month, like the female menstrual cycle and about as pleasant.

Last Saturday evening was typical. Like clockwork, at 6:00 p.m. my mother screamed up to me, "Dress the right way." "Of course, mama," I responded, while thinking that I might wear my black lace bra and panties, or maybe go down totally naked with a sign saying "TAKE ME NOW, PLEASE!" But I once more put on my plain-Jane outfit, which makes me look like . . . well, a cross between Marie Osmond and the Virgin Mary. "Damn!" I thought. "There's the bell. It's showtime!"

As usual, dinner was served at 6:15. Benny tore vigorously at his chicken, reminding me of a wolf with its prey. It was disgusting, but no one said anything, and Benny just sighed with pleasure as he devoured the last piece. Speaking fast, with much upper-body motion, Rosa gossiped with my mother about everyone they know. For some reason, Rosa reminds me of a dog in heat. "Oh God," I groaned inwardly, "do I have a headache!" At last dinner was over. As my mother started to clear the table, Benny lit a cigar (I hate cigars) and leaned over toward me. The following conversation ensued.

"So, what do you go to school for, Sandrina?"

"I go to school to study and learn, Benito."

"And what is it that you learn there?" he asked suspiciously. I felt like saying, "I learn that idiots like you are not worth my time." But I said, "I'm majoring in English, Benito. I want to be a teacher."

"A teacher? Hmmm. That's a nice little job for a girl."

Wham, bang, pow! I nearly exploded inside. I wanted to say, "Hey, Benny, what the hell is your brain made of, cottage cheese? Kitty litter? Doggie-do?" But a proper Italian girl would never say such a thing. I let Benny continue.

"You know, Tony. I don't understand why you send your daughter to school. A girl who goes to school needs a car. When she gets a car, who knows what she'll do. Before you know it, she's running around with all sorts of people. No, a girl only needs to go to school until she is sixteen, because that's the law here. Then she should be taken to Italy, found a nice boy, and married off to him. That's my philosophy."

So there you have it, Benito's philosophy of raising a daughter. At least, my father said nothing. But Benito didn't look for an answer. He just sat there smiling, totally content with himself, as though he had put everything to rights with his profound philosophical discourse. You know, the way a guy looks the morning after he's lost his virginity.

SANDRA CALVI

Organized chronologically and telling a story about people and events, this is a full-fledged narrative essay—that is, an essay that consists of narration from beginning to end. Narration can also be used in an essay in passing, to exemplify a point, perhaps, or flesh out an argument. Indeed, narration can be a powerful tool. Let me tell you a story of how I learned the power of narration:

A teenager at the time, I was alone in a huge house in a foreign city; it was midnight; unable to sleep, I went downstairs and pulled a book from a bookcase shelf—Poe's *Murders in the Rue Morgue*; I read it through and was literally scared stiff; I couldn't move for terror; next morning I awoke in the chair in which I had read Poe's gripping tale.

Now, there was a narrative passage in an otherwise non-narrative context, a passage serving to exemplify. Such passages are to be found in a great many essays, even the most formal (like Ph.D. dissertations). For, as I've said, narrative examples can carry particular weight. Why? Because we are physical creatures in a physical world, creatures who can never fully grasp what is shapeless—ideas, feelings—unless somehow related to the perceptual world of experience. I think you will agree with me that the abstraction "narration can be a powerful means of communicating" by itself does not communicate nearly as strongly or fully as my little story about being scared stiff. And that's the point.

Anyway, people like narration and find it interesting. People generally feel that narrative examples spice up a piece of writing and help make it enjoyable. That's why narration can be a good way of leading the reader into an essay or of creating a strong ending. We've dealt with a number of ways to begin and to end. Here is yet another way to accomplish the one or the other. For instance, take my little Poe experience again. An essay on the power of narration could begin with the story and move immediately to the thesis (a funnel structure) thus:

Story: [As given previously]

Bridge: This just goes to show how potent narration can be with regard to the reader's feelings.

Thesis: Indeed, narration is one of the most powerful tools a writer has.

Here is how the same incident might be used to end an essay:

Bridge: Narration, then, clearly has much power over us human beings. But I've known this for a long while. Let me tell you the story of how I learned the power of narration.

Story: [As given previously]

Now, what about you? You have a world of experiences stored up in you. Tap into that world as you write, using noteworthy incidents in your life to exemplify and argue your points. Beginning writers rarely make use of the wealth they possess—their experiences in life and the knowledge that has come with experience. As a result, their writing, even if coherent, tends to be pallid, lacking the sense of immediacy and the vibrancy of which they are capable. When you write your next paper, try incorporating a relevant incident or two from your life. You will find that your discussion comes alive and your writing is more than just readable—it's interesting as well.

DIALOGUE AND FICTIONAL DETAIL

It's possible to write a whole essay in the form of dialogue. Witness Plato, whose dialogues are among the greatest philosophical works ever written. Dialogue is most often used, however, as Sandra Calvi uses it in "So Much for Philosophy!"—that is, incidentally. The essay as a whole is narrative, but it is enlivened by the dialogue, which captures the personalities of the people described. Whenever dialogue is appropriate—and it can be in almost any kind of writing—its use can strengthen an essay by giving it solidity and a sense of authenticity.

Certainly, Ms. Calvi's dialogue does just that. By giving us Benito in his own words, she says what she has to say in a way that we can relate to immediately. But, you may wonder, is everything we're told Benito said true? Did the writer write down every word as he was talking? If not, this essay is at least partly fiction. But if it's fiction, how can it be an essay? The answer is that, in fact, so-called "nonfictional" prose is not always— and need not always be—factual. Just as there are historical novels that are in large measure factual, there are essays that are in part or sometimes even entirely fictional. To be sure, if a writer expects the reader to accept a piece as purely factual, as do historians and biographers, then to make things up—even bits of dialogue—would be irresponsible. The reader would have a right to feel duped. But in an essay like Calvi's, it really doesn't matter one way or the other. The only thing that really matters is the point and its being put across forcefully and enjoyably. Everything else is a means to that end.

In other words, don't be afraid to use fictional details in your writing if they will help get your point across forcefully and enjoyably. Of course, if it will matter to your reader whether something is factual, then it should be factual, or you should alert your readers to the fact that the dialogue they're about to read, or your description of a place, or the character sketch you're going to draw is imagined. For instance, should you write a paper on Grant and Lee in which you have a hypothetical dialogue between the two, you should introduce the passage by saying something like, "We can only imagine what Grant and Lee said at Appomattox. Here is what I imagine they said." By so doing, you would manage to get in your fictional dialogue without any possibility of misleading anyone. But if it doesn't matter whether something is factual, then don't worry about it. Use whatever means you like to achieve your end. In this case, the end entirely justifies the means.

TONE AND VOICE

Every essay should be "heard" by the reader as if it were spoken by someone. That is, every essay conveys a sense of the voice of its speaker—a sense of a particular person expressing a particular attitude. The tone of voice can run the gamut from warm and friendly to aloof and condescending. We've had a good example of tone and the sense of voice already in "So Much for Philosophy!" In fact, this essay makes its point mainly through its tone. That is, what we are meant to understand about Benito and everything he represents is communicated primarily through the mocking tone of the essay's speaker, whose voice seems that of a lively but disgruntled (not without cause) young woman.

Especially instructive with regard to tone and voice is the kind of essay whose speaker is to be taken as a fictional character, as opposed to the author speaking in all earnestness. Most writing, to be sure, is intended to be heard as spoken by the author; and so readers generally and rightly identify the speaker and the author, attributing the speaker's attitude to the author. But some essays are not meant to be taken in this way. In order to create a fictional speaker with a voice appropriate to the writer's purpose—stuffy, perhaps, or naive, or malevolent, or insane—the writer must choose and manipulate words and sentence patterns carefully. In this type of essay, then, the deliberateness of the writer with regard to word choice and sentence patterns is crucial—which is why this type of essay is particularly instructive. Consider, for instance, the following from Jonathan Swift's "A Modest Proposal," the classic example of a piece of exposition with a fictional speaker:

> I have been assured by a very knowing American of my acquaintance in London, that a young healthy child well nursed is at a year old a most delicious, nourishing and wholesome food, whether stewed, roasted, baked, or boiled, and I make no doubt that it will equally serve in a fricassee, or a ragout.
>
> I do therefore humbly offer it to public consideration, that of the hundred and twenty thousand children already computed, twenty thousand may be reserved for breed, whereof only one fourth part to be males, which is more than we allow to sheep, black-cattle, or swine, and my reason is that these children are seldom the fruits of marriage, a circumstance not much regarded by our savages, therefore one male will be sufficient to serve four females. That the remaining hundred thousand may at a year old be offered in sale to the persons of quality, and fortune, through the kingdom, always advising the mother to let them suck plentifully in the last month, so as to render them plump, and fat for a good table. A child will make two dishes at an entertainment for friends, and when the family dines alone, the fore or hind quarter will make a reasonable dish, and seasoned with a little pepper or salt will be very good boiled on the fourth day, especially in winter.

This passage is not meant to be taken as spoken by Swift. Rather, we are to hear the voice of an imaginary bureaucrat who has lost sight of human values in his abstract musings about governmental problems and solutions (bureaucrats in the eighteenth century were not unlike those we know and love). The point of the essay, thus, is ironic, opposite from any point its speaker makes. But my point is that the tone and voice of "A Modest Proposal" were carefully crafted by Swift for a purpose. The ordinary vocabulary of the passage and its simple (for the eighteenth century) phrasing produce a matter-of-fact tone, a tone reinforced by the understatement and lack of emotion in the passage. But the tone is entirely wrong for the horrendous subject matter. Is this the voice of insanity, one wonders? Yes, it is, and that's the point: Swift crafted the tone and voice of the essay to suggest dramatically the insanity that so often governs our lawmakers, who so often focus on expediency rather than rectitude.

What we've noted about "A Modest Proposal"—that its tone and voice were crafted for a purpose—is no less true of any professional writing, though it's easy to lose sight of this fact. An accomplished writer chooses words, sentence patterns, and so forth with the aim of creating a posture, or stance, that is exactly right for the subject matter and the purpose at hand. With this fact in mind, read the following passage from E. M. Forster's essay "Tolerance" and determine what its tone is and the qualities of its voice, or of the person speaking the passage. Determine, too, whether or not its tone and voice are appropriate and effective with respect to what is being said. Then read the second passage—my rewrite—and contrast its effect with Forster's. Why did Forster *choose* the kind of words and sentence patterns he did rather than those of my rewrite?

> The world is very full of people—appallingly full; it has never been so full before—and they are all tumbling over each other. Most of these people one doesn't know and some of them one doesn't like; doesn't like the color of their skins, say, or the shapes of their noses, or the way they blow them or don't blow them, or the way they talk, or their smell, or their clothes, or their fondness for jazz or their dislike of jazz, and so on. Well, what is one to do? There are two solutions. One of them is the Nazi solution. If you don't like people, kill them, banish them, segregate them, and then strut up and down proclaiming that you are the salt of the earth. The other way is much less thrilling, but it is on the whole the way of the democracies, and I prefer it. If you don't like people, put up with them as well as you can. Don't try to love them; you can't, you'll only strain yourself. But try to tolerate them. On the basis of that tolerance a civilized future may

be built. Certainly I can see no other foundation for the post-war world.

The world is vastly overpopulated—appallingly so; grotesquely overburdened with multitudes of *homo sapiens* as never before—and they interfere with each other in their diurnal endeavors. One is acquainted with only a minuscule fraction of these hominoids, and some of those of whom one is cognizant, one does not care for; does not care for the hue of their skin-tones, perhaps, or the dimensions of their prosboscises, or how they expel or do not expel air through their nostrils to clear them, or the way they expostulate, or their odors, or their garments, or their liking or disliking music of a popular cast, et cetera. What, one may well ponder, is one's response to this situation to be, this situation in which one finds oneself helplessly enmeshed, hopelessly mired; and, though one tries to keep one's sense of perspective, that sense seems impossible to maintain, eroding, as it does, in proportion to one's proximity to one or another population center? Having perused the problem carefully and for some duration, I find there to be—and believe the reader will assent to my conclusion—two possible resolutions to the situation with which we are confronted, nay, two and only two practicable solutions: we must either endure these hordes in patience or, in Conrad's memorable phrase, "Exterminate the brutes." [Which do you think the speaker of this passage would be for?]

The language of the Forster passage is that of ordinary good English, fairly plain and yet eloquent in a soft-spoken way. Together with a gently wry kind of humor—for instance, "you'll only strain yourself"—Forster's language establishes the voice of an open, friendly, engaging person speaking to the reader as a friend, a voice that itself seems tolerant and so one that lends Forster's argument credence and authority. In contrast, the voice of the rewrite is persnickety, aloof, frigid to the core. Content has been held constant; the difference is solely a matter of word choice throughout and sentence structure toward the end. But what a difference! Just compare Forster's "they are all tumbling over each other" and "they interfere with each other" of the rewrite. The latter abstraction sounds disengaged and official; because of the charming concretion "tumbling," the original seems warm and engaging.

Differences like these are not accidental; they result from deliberation and choice with regard to words and grammatical structure. Of course, to attain the high degree of consciousness and skill required for such deliberation takes time and much practice. But you can start now simply by reading everything you write aloud and listening for the tone(s) and the kind of voice you have created. Anything you write will exhibit both; you just have to learn to hear them. And you will if you listen hard enough. Then, you will get these important aspects of exposition under your control—important because they very much shape the reader's feelings and reception. You might also try your hand at forging a speaker other than yourself. I've found with my own students that writing essays with fictional speakers helps distance them and so allows them to see what must be done to fashion a voice for a given purpose. And anyway, it's fun to write an essay like this and even therapeutic. One can take out all kinds of frustrations, for instance, by creating a terribly nasty voice for a person one dislikes while learning more about writing at the same time. That seems a bargain to me.

THE CHARACTER SKETCH

Because more often than not essays concern people, the character sketch is a common element of exposition, one frequently used along the way to provide an example or to flesh out an idea by giving the reader a sense of the person whose idea it is (or was). Indeed, because most people find people to be fascinating in themselves, an entire essay can be given over to a character sketch of a specific person, real or imagined, or of a type of person in general, as the following essay exemplifies. The writer, note, has adopted the voice and style of a child.

My Best Friend

Yesterday we were playing in the park, Jessy and me. She's my best friend in the whole world. Her mommy and daddy drove us. All the kids were there—Jimmy, Sally, Cara, Andy. Their mommies and daddies were with them. Mine weren't. My mommy and daddy don't live with each other any more.

There're all these things happening at my house now. My mommy quit her job and went to drive all around the United States by herself. She just told me one day that she had to go away for a while and not to be sad and she loved me. I don't get it. I guess I was bad.

So now daddy and me live alone. Well, not really alone.

There's a woman who lives with us who pretends to be my mommy and her cats and baby named Noel, just because she was born on Christmas. Isn't that silly? She cries all the time—loud. Daddy loves her and talks to her all the time. He doesn't talk to me much anymore. I guess when you're nearly seven you're too big.

We used to have a lot of fun, mommy and me. We'd play for hours or go to the zoo and see the monkeys and tigers and everything except snakes. I hate snakes. Sometimes she'd stay home from work and we'd make up games like cowgirls or famous women.

Daddy has too many rules and you have to be quiet all the time. And I have to be nice to Noel and her mommy whenever daddy's there. There aren't any games anymore.

Anyway, as I was saying, Jessy is my best friend. We play together all the time. If I didn't have Jessy, I don't know what I'd do. I go over to her house and we play with our babies—Jessy just got Dream Baby and I have Cuddles. And we talk, Jessy and me. I tell her how sad I am and how I would like to be her sister. I wish it would never be time to go home.

When I get home, I go to my room. I miss my mommy the most at bedtime, when she would tuck me in and sing a song. But I tell myself that I have to be a big girl now. So I pull the covers over my head, hug my teddy, and try to think about happy things so I'll have good dreams when I fall asleep.

JENNIFER CARROLL

Note the use of detail here. What brings this character sketch of its imagined speaker to life is the details. With this in mind, try writing a character sketch of your own. See if you can't build a person detail by detail, rendering the feel of what it's like to be that person. Then carry over that sense of detail to everything you write. By so doing you will develop a habit of mind that will serve you well by keeping your writing concrete and thus vivid and immediate.

SYMBOLISM

Though we usually associate symbolism with fiction and poetry, symbols are to be found in every nook and cranny of human life—a symbol being simply anything that in a given context means something different from (though usually related to) its literal meaning. In the 1960s, for example, hair was symbolic, suggesting a political viewpoint. In fact, hair and clothing are usually symbolic in that we express ourselves through the styles we choose, intending to reflect the intangibles of personality through the tangible—even if we're not always conscious of our symbolic intent.

At any rate, conscious and deliberate symbolism may be as much an aspect of nonfiction prose as it is of fiction and poetry. For instance, setting can function symbolically in essays just as it can in fiction. That is, the particular time and/or place spoken of in an essay might be more than just a backdrop; setting can provide symbolic commentary. Consider the first paragraph of a marvelously concrete essay entitled "Bureaucrats," by Joan Didion:

> The closed door upstairs at 120 South Spring Street in downtown Los Angeles is marked OPERATIONS CENTER. In the windowless room beyond the closed door a reverential hush prevails. From six a.m. until seven p.m. in this windowless room men sit at consoles watching a huge board flash colored lights. "There's the heart attack," someone will murmur, or "we're getting the gawk effect." 120 South Spring is the Los Angeles office of Caltrans, or the California Department of Transportation, and the Operations Center is where Caltrans engineers monitor what they call "the 42-Mile Loop." . . . The windowless room at 120 South Spring is where incidents get "verified." "Incident verification" is turning on the closed-circuit TV on the console and watching the traffic slow down to see (this is "the gawk effect") where the Camaro tore out the fence.

Caltrans is a closed system shut off from the real world, as are bureaucracies in general, Didion is suggesting. This is what the "closed door" and especially the "windowless room" come to symbolize if we pay close attention to the details of the passage. In "Bureaucrats," the setting provides a backdrop and much more: finally, it makes a symbolic statement about Caltrans and similar bureaucracies. But it does so concretely, through images we can relate to. And such is the great advantage that symbolism affords: it allows a writer to speak of things that are intangible and abstract, having no physical form—like bureaucracy or patriotism or ideas about love or home—palpably, concretely, immediately through the senses.

METAPHORICAL LANGUAGE

Narration, dialogue, perceptual details, tone and voice, the character sketch, and symbols are all ways of making writing concrete, for in one way or another they all involve the senses, either through the imagination (like a story) or directly (like tone and voice). When we read a narrative passage or essay, we imaginatively *see* someone somewhere doing something; when we fully read a piece of exposition, we *hear* a human voice and its various tones. Genuine communication can take place only when the whole being of the reader is engaged and not just the intellect alone. Why should this be so? Because we are physical creatures in a physical world, creatures who can never fully grasp what is shapeless—ideas, feelings—when not related to the perceptual world of experience. Therefore, the things that are concrete about writing are not mere ornaments to deck out the meaning but are central to that meaning, are necessary to the goal of communication.

Thus it is that the best writers use all of the methods just listed and others as well to gain concreteness. Whatever it is you're writing, then, be as concrete as possible; never keep your reader in the thin air of abstraction for more than a few sentences running. Note my metaphor—"thin air of abstraction"—and how it makes my point about abstraction immediate, easy to grasp.

A metaphor is a figurative expression that entails an analogy between essentially *unlike* things. It is the essential unlikeness of the things compared that makes a phrase figurative (as opposed to literal) in the first place. So, for instance, "John is a lot like his brother Seth" is literal—because the things compared are essentially alike—and not figurative, and so not metaphorical. In contrast, "the children made pigs of themselves" involves an analogy between things essentially different; therefore, the expression is figurative, the specific figure being metaphor. In sum, there are literal analogies and there are figurative analogies. The latter we call *metaphors* and *similes* (a simile is simply a metaphor underscored by the use of "as" or "like").

Metaphors may be either explicit or implicit. In an explicit metaphor, both terms of the analogy are stated. Some examples are: "*solitude* is the *salt* of personhood," "the *woman* is a *dynamo*," "my *love* is like a *flea*." In an implicit metaphor, one term of the analogy is not stated but somehow implied. For example, every time we speak of "feeding the computer," we're making an implicit analogy between it and a living creature; when we speak of "spending time," we're making an implicit analogy between time and money (which are linked by the explicit metaphor "time is money"); and should you feel "wounded" by what someone has said, then what was said is implicitly a knife or other weapon.

Both explicit and implicit metaphors can be either discrete or extended. A discrete metaphor is any metaphor used once and left at that. An extended metaphor is one that is developed over a passage or even an entire essay. Here is a piece built on an extended metaphor, that of fire. All the metaphorical words are printed in italics. Follow the metaphor through, observing how it helps to structure the piece and give a sense of forward motion.

The Feud Burns On

When I was nine years old, I went to our neighbor's house to play ball. We were having fun until trouble *flared* between me and Bob, the neighbor's son. I was running with the ball when Bob stuck out his leg and tripped me. Blood oozing from my nose, I stood up *raging*, and punched Bob in the nose. We fought until separated by his parents. Bob blamed me for the fight and I blamed him. But whoever was responsible, this incident *sparked* a feud between our families that has *burned* for many years.

Even now, over ten years later, the animosity between us continues to *smolder*. Whenever I see Bob or anyone in his family, I look the other way. And they reciprocate. My parents, too, never speak to them or even of them. The *flame* of hatred can still *burn bright*. Nothing now, I think, could *extinguish* this feud.

TERENCE MULGREW

Some Pitfalls of Metaphor

However potentially powerful, metaphor can backfire if not thought through. There are many ways in which you can go wrong using metaphors and, therefore, you should be alert to many things when using them.

For one thing, get rid of any trite metaphors that creep into your writing. Many metaphors have been used so often that they no longer do anything other than to deaden one's prose. Such metaphors as "clear as crystal," "white as a sheet," and "ran like the wind" do the opposite of what metaphors should do. Pale and worn, they are so familiar that they lend no verbal force at all. Also, avoid metaphors that are strained or that call undue attention to themselves: for example, "like a boiling lobster, the sky turned from black to red." Not only is this metaphor strained, but it also brings up feelings and associations that are not relevant to a simple description of the changing colors of a sky and that work against the desired mood. The careful writer looks at metaphors from every angle and discards any with aberrant implications in the given context—like boiling to death here.

Then, be on the lookout for mixed metaphor—that is, the piling up of discrete metaphors that don't fit well together: "Now is the time to take a stand in the public eye"; "Afraid that she would never reach the top of the heap, Elsa dived into her studies, determined not to give up before the first round even began." In the first instance, the poor public is having its eye put out; in the second, Elsa, a very agile girl indeed, dives from a heap while boxing. When visualized, these metaphors are ludicrous in context with each other. Because metaphors have a way of linking up, watch what happens between them. The result of not watching metaphorical linkages and implications carefully is usually a descent into nonsense. Extended metaphors, especially, can easily become mixed. When you extend a metaphor, make sure to stay in the same area for all metaphorical terms. The following goes wrong because the area from which the third metaphorical term is drawn is different from that of the first two terms: "Their struggle for power was like a prize fight between two champion heavyweights; and when one lowered his guard, the other scored the deciding goal." For the metaphor to work, it must be extended thus: "the other delivered the knockout punch."

Finally, be alert to the little quirks of language and, because of odd linkages, avoid using metaphor at all in certain contexts: for example, "Consumers beware! The water company is trying to bleed us dry!"; "Mrs. Johnson married an old flame, who managed to burn down her house on their wedding night." These sentences, both from newspapers, don't contain mixed metaphors as such; but a literal statement in context with a figurative statement can sometimes be ludicrous—as are the linkages of "water" and "bleed," "flame" and "burn." Both sentences would have been far better if the metaphor in each had been restated in literal language. I can't resist quoting two more like sentences, which further exemplify the need for caution when using figurative language: "It is indeed an honor to sit beside the giants upon whose shoulders we stand";

"'As a student,' Professor Marsh said, 'Maynard was in a class by himself.'"

In sum, there is a logic to metaphor that the writer must respect. There are many pitfalls for the unwary with regard to metaphor, but nothing carries as much power as the right metaphor in the right place.

SOUND AND RHYTHM

We think of images, metaphors, narratives, and so forth as concrete because they can be imagined in all their solidity. But sound and rhythm are still more concrete and immediate, for neither needs to be imagined: sounds we hear directly with our ears and rhythms we feel directly in our muscles.

Take these two sentences from Claire McMahon's "My Summer Job" (page 86):

. . . the salary was terrible: five dollars for bowing to bitches.

"Hubby" was sneaking a squeeze of my newly chubby behind.

These sentences are full of harsh sounds: the *t, d, b,* and *ch* sounds of the first; the *s, k, q, ch,* and *b* sounds of the second. We might note, too, the ironic *hubby/chubby* rhyme. In concentration, these sounds produce a tone of derision and disgust, a tone that some other way of saying the same things would not: for instance, "My earnings were small: five dollars for smiling at mean old women." Clearly, it is the sound more than the meaning that creates the derisive tone of McMahon's sentences. Such is what I mean by special effect.

Rhythm in prose is usually a matter not of sentences but of whole paragraphs or even larger units. When critics speak of *prose rhythm*, they mean the rhythm that a passage as a whole creates. Here, for instance, are two passages from the same essay—Lewis Thomas's "Late Night Thoughts on Listening to Mahler's Ninth Symphony"—that are markedly different in rhythm, the difference reflecting the difference in the speaker's feelings about his topics. See if you can determine what kind of rhythm emerges from each passage and perhaps even how the rhythm of each is created.

I cannot listen to Mahler's Ninth Symphony with anything like the old melancholy mixed with the high pleasure I used to take from this music. There was a time, not long ago, when what I heard, especially in the final movement, was an open acknowledgment of death and at the same time a quiet celebration of the tranquillity connected to the process. I took this music as a metaphor for reassurance, confirming my own strong hunch that the dying of every living creature, the most natural of all experiences, has to be a peaceful experience. I rely on nature. The long passages on all the strings at the end, as close as music can come to expressing silence itself, I used to hear as Mahler's idea of leave-taking at its best. But always, I have heard this music as a solitary, private listener, thinking about death.

• • •

Now all that has changed. I cannot think that way anymore. Not while those things are still in place, aimed everywhere, ready for launching.

This is a bad enough thing for the people in my generation. We can put up with it, I suppose, since we must. We are moving along anyway, like it or not. I can even set aside my private fancy about hanging around, in midair.

What I cannot imagine, what I cannot put up with, the thought that keeps grinding its way into my mind, making the Mahler into a hideous noise close to killing me, is what it would be like to be young. How do the young stand it? How can they keep their sanity? If I were very young, sixteen or seventeen years old, I think I would begin, perhaps very slowly and imperceptibly, to go crazy.

With its long, complex sentences—as long as the "passages on all the strings" in Mahler's Ninth are said to be—the first passage is slow, meditative, graceful in its forward motion. The mind here is at its ease. In contrast, the second passage, which is composed of very short simple sentences or sentences built from short compounded phrases and clauses, is choppy, halting, irritable in its movement as well as its sentiment. Clearly, rhythm is an intimate part of Lewis's meaning, or of the way he means.

You may or you may not think much about rhythm as you continue to write. After all, it's not a crucial consideration even in good writing. That's true, except for endings. There is a rhythm of closure, and to master it will help you attain something that is always difficult to attain but always of value in terms of an essay's effect on its readers—an ending that feels like an ending. Take the last paragraph of Sandra Calvi's "So Much for Philosophy!" at the beginning of this chapter.

So there you have it, Benito's philosophy of raising a daughter. At least, my father said nothing. But Benito didn't look for an answer. He just sat there smiling, totally content with himself, as though he had put everything to rights with his profound philosophical discourse. You know, the way a guy looks the morning after he's lost his virginity.

Now read the paragraph again, but this time stop before the last sentence. To my ear, the paragraph and thus the essay would seem truncated without that last sentence. The sentence is needed not for the meaning, really, but for the sake of closure. In part through the image it creates but especially through its rapid pace, the last sentence gives the essay that sense of an ending I spoke of in the last chapter.

TITLES

The title of a paper is the first thing a reader sees, what first focuses the reader's attention and thinking. Therefore, titles are psychologically important and should not be neglected. But what makes for a good title? A student paragraph we considered earlier (page 32) puts the matter well: "a really good title ... must satisfy two very different criteria: first, it should not mislead the reader (this is the ethical demand); yet, second, it should be imaginative. In other words, *a good title should both inform and delight.*" Following are several types of title (which overlap to some degree). Before titling your next paper, you might consider whether one of these types would be effective.

1. A title may simply indicate the topic of an essay: "The Jaspers," "Rushing," "My Summer Job." By raising the question "What about it?" this type of title draws the reader to the essay's thesis statement, which provides the answer.

2. A title may point directly to a thesis (without exactly stating it) or to the conclusion drawn from arguing the thesis: "Organizational Cultures: A Contrast" does the former; "The Problem of Choice," the latter. In each case, the title clarifies what the author deems central to the essay as it unfolds.

3. Some titles are "grabbers," grabbing our attention and piquing our curiosity: "So Much for Philosophy!" and "The Feud Burns

On" fit this category. Titles that prove to be ironic with respect to the essays they head are also grabbers, albeit in retrospect: "My Summer Job," for instance, is such a title in that its mundaneness is in sharp contrast with the tone and liveliness of the essay as it unfolds. The discrepancy seems delightfully ironic as it becomes apparent.

4. A title may be metaphorical or symbolic, distilling an essay's meaning into a single image. "The Feud Burns On" is an example.

THEME AND THESIS

Earlier chapters have stated often that almost all papers of the kind done in college have a thesis. (What a thesis is you already know: it is what an essay that argues a thesis argues, what its support material supports, what gives such an essay point and focus.) This is the kind of essay we have focused on in the first four chapters of this book—the essay that begins with a thesis statement and then brings evidence to bear to support that statement. However, there is a second kind of essay, one that does not expound a thesis but instead conveys and supports a theme.

The difference between a thesis and a theme is overtness: theses are stated; themes are implied. At the end of the first (funnel) paragraph of Tracy Masucci's "A Matter of Face" (page 85), for instance, comes a fully stated thesis: "A person's normal facial expression . . . can tell a great deal about that person generally." The rest of the essay consists of examples demonstrating the point. In contrast, Sandra Calvi's "So Much for Philosophy!" and Jennifer Carroll's "My Best Friend" (both from this chapter) contain themes. Nowhere in either is a statement of thesis to be found; nevertheless, each clearly makes a point. Narrative essays and essays entirely given over to sketching a character are usually thematic, whereas more formal essays—like the term paper—almost always entail a thesis, which is why we have focused on the latter. Still, you should be aware of both types and decide what type you will write according to your purpose and subject.

EXERCISES

1. Write a narrative essay—one that tells a story—that includes some dialogue and a character sketch. Be sure to have a point in mind, but now imply it instead of stating it.

2. Write a short paper with a speaker other than you. You could put your speaker into a situation to which he or she is responding, or you could have your speaker make a proposal of some sort, or you could have him or her defend a cause, to mention just a few possibilities. Remember, whatever your speaker's point, your purpose will be to reveal something about your speaker in part through what is said but even more through how it is said. Through the kind of words you choose and the kind of grammatical structures you use, fashion the right tone and the right kind of voice for your speaker.

3. Do what is assigned in Exercise 2, except now write an essay in dialogue form between two speakers, neither of whom is you. You might, for instance, make a point through a dialogue between a professor and a student in class discussion, or between your mother or father and your sister or brother on a matter regarding you. Try to create different voices for the two speakers you pick by way of the kind of words and grammatical structures you choose for each speaker.

4. Write a character sketch, or at least a piece that contains one, like Sandra Calvi's "So Much for Philosophy" (page 100). You may wish to be satirical, as is Calvi, or you could write a nonsatirical sketch.

5. Some of the following sentences contain trite metaphors; some contain mixed metaphors; and some contain blanks to be filled in from the phrases that follow. Spot the trite metaphors, correct the mixed metaphors, and fill in each blank with a metaphorical phrase appropriate to the given sentence.

   a. When terrorists jumped onto the stage, silence reigned in the hall and the lecturer turned white as a sheet.

   b. Harold plunged into his work, hoping that with enough effort he could
   _____.
   (1) get out of his difficulties
   (2) scramble to the top
   (3) keep his head above water
   (4) learn to float

   c. The government has a stranglehold on the nation's economy, crippling growth with regulations and stifling investment with new taxes.

   d. Owing money to everyone she knew, Terry was immersed in _____ of debt.
   (1) a mountain
   (2) an ocean
   (3) a lot
   (4) a stream

e. Accused of being green with envy, Sam turned as red as a beet.

f. Mr. Waxwing stooped to nothing except when it came to social climbing.

g. "That was the straw that broke the camel's back," John said as he searched the room, looking for a needle in a haystack.

h. Like an old hand navigating a tricky river, Sally _____, and then it was smooth sailing all the way.
(1) climbed to the top of the heap
(2) beat off the competition
(3) negotiated the rapids of her profession
(4) hit a homer

i. Because he was as cold as ice, Daniel was as slow as molasses in getting to school this morning.

j. Like some wild animal, Hillis bounded down the field; but he was finally pinned at the ten-yard line.

6. A metaphor is extended over the course of the following essay. Determine what that metaphor is and then trace the extension paragraph by paragraph. Consider, too, what the extension serves to do in the essay and whether the extension is successfully carried out.

Body and Soul

It's 2:30 on Sunday afternoon and I'm listening to music. Not just any music: *this* is the "New York Citizens," live, so live that I can feel Mike's drum beats and Paul's bass guitar notes pounding away in my chest like a second heartbeat. With every beat, a monologue of notes bursts lightly from Dan's electric guitar. Rob's lead-singing voice—now harsh, like cheap whiskey; now rich and sweet, like hot chocolate—reverberates in my head. I can't say a word: there are men at work. Or, rather, *man* at work, for as a band, these musicians are one musical body and soul.

Mike is the heart of the band. Ticking his drumsticks together, he starts each song. He controls the music's flow by setting the tempo. When he speeds up, so does the rest of the band. Without a drummer, the music would lose its beat. Without Mike, the body would have no pulse.

Paul and Dan are the skeleton of the band. Paul, on bass

guitar, sets a base line, a melodic version of the drumbeat, supporting the music's main melody. Dan plays that main melody on lead guitar. The main melody gives the music form. Without bass and lead guitars, the music would have no structure. Without Paul and Dan, the body would have no backbone.

Rob is the song writer of the band and its lead singer. His music reflects his words; his words dance to his music. Together, Rob's words and music give the band purpose. They breathe life into the body, which otherwise would be inanimate. Without Rob, there would be no soul.

One musical body and soul—that's what this band is, at least on its best days. And today is one of those days. I've never heard them play as well as they are now playing. They lift my soul and animate my body. I could go on, but that's enough. Shhh. I want to listen.

P. J. Levins

7. Get out some old papers of yours and read them aloud. Catch the sound and rhythm of your words, pausing whenever you hear something you like or something that seems awkward, harsh, somehow unpleasant. Try to determine what it is you like and why you like it. As to passages whose sound and/or rhythm seems unmeaningfully jarring, try to rewrite them so as to get rid of configurations that unduly call attention to themselves. While you're at it, you might look at the titles of your old papers. What kind of title is each? What does each do? What ones seem effective and what ones don't? Why? The reason for looking at old papers in these ways is that they are old and, therefore, distanced. It's easier to see what you're distanced from. But, of course, the object of looking at old papers is to be better able to see what you're doing at present. Try, then, to apply what you learn from looking at your past writing to the writing you do from here on out.

Style

Generally speaking, style is the cumulative by-product of all the choices made by a writer and the effects of those choices. One writer writes a narrative essay full of descriptive details and metaphors, an essay that, in effect, is rich and sensuous; another presents a thesis and supports it with definitions and examples, this second essay being highly intellectual in effect. These are all matters of style or stylistic choice. Specifically, style is the cumulative result of the choices a writer makes with regard to diction and to syntax, both of which are instrumental in shaping tone and voice, along with the effects of these choices. These—diction and syntax—are the subjects of this chapter.

DICTION

Diction refers to the kind of words chosen. There are many categories of words: for instance, some words are abstract and some concrete (*an edible* versus *a juicy* steak); some are literal and some metaphorical (*the expanse of the sea* versus *the undulant body of the sea*); some are almost strictly denotative and some richly connotative (*domicile* versus *home*); some are slangy and some are formal (*it's a drag* versus *it is quite tedious*); and so forth. Also, we speak of levels of diction, meaning that some words are appropriate in some situations and not others. Words can be divided into three levels: informal, ordinary, and formal. Informal diction, which includes slang, covers the kind of words we use in private with friends, in private journals, perhaps, or in personal letters. Ordinary diction is the diction we use every day with people with whom we are not intimate but are still friendly, like our teachers, and is generally the diction of college papers. And formal diction is that of ceremonial occasions, such as funerals, as well as of dissertations and writing in the professions generally. The principle is this: the kind of words one uses on Saturday night with friends is not the kind one uses on Sunday morning as one accompanies one's grandmother to church.

Different types of diction contribute to stylistic difference. For instance, a diction that is highly metaphorical would probably result in a style that could be called *poetic*, whereas a diction that is mainly abstract and literal would result in a style best described as *prosaic*. Informal, ordinary, and formal diction tend to be characteristic of, respectively, the informal style of personal letters; the ordinary, or middle, style of most public speech and writing; and the formal style of funeral orations and research papers. These categories almost always overlap—or are mixed for special effect—in any given piece of prose.

Here are two essays that, like most of the samples in this book, were written by students. As you read them, consider what kinds of diction and what styles they exemplify.

Party Buddies

I became a party buddy last weekend at an uptown Irish bar. For I possess the one virtue needed under the circumstance.

"Dude-man, you're Irish, aren't you?" I was asked.

"Uh, yeah, Irish-American," I answered.

"AWRIGHT!" my interrogator shot back. "What county?"

"Um, Nassau," I replied, referring to my parent's home on Long Island.

As question marks appeared above my compatriot's head, I kind of regretted my aloofness. He may have been ignorant, but he was friendly. Hadn't he referred to me as "brother" in between the repeated slaps on my back? So, though my impulse was to bail out, I stuck around as he tried to explain to another brother exactly where in Boston he came from.

"No, Dude, not there!" he yelled. "That's niggertown."

I hit the street, cursing myself for not trusting my first instinct. As I walked, I wondered: Are any of these third and fourth generation American Celtics any more Irish than the basketball team that goes by that name? Does the mere fact that we have ancestors from the same island make this racist my brother? What is the nature of the bond between party buddies?

As to the last question, I'm sure that they must have a like ancestry, be it Italian, German, or Spanish. Party buddies are not only Irish-Americans; they are found in all ethnic groups. Then, to be a party buddy, one must be or at least appear to be as stupid as one's buddy. If you seem stupid enough, you are declared "brother." If you seem stupid and crack a beer, you are "Bud brothers" (or Bud-dies). And if, in your stupidity, you smoke a spliff, you are "doobie brothers." Third, then, you must drink and/or smoke along with your buddy. This buddy system always entails a false sense of camaraderie-induced-by-mood-altering-substances. Finally, and most important, you must behave in such a way and say whatever is necessary to convince your "friend" that you share beliefs entirely and that your mutual world view is entirely correct. Party buddies want to believe that theirs is the only valid way of life.

And if that way is somehow questioned, they can turn on a dime. For instance, take my "dude-man" buddy of the other night. As I got up to leave, he said, "Where ya going? You offended by something?"

Lying through my teeth, I said, "Naw, I just gotta get home."

"Bull," he said, "you took offense at what I said. I can see it now. You're a goddamned . . . abolitionist!" He turned away and moved down the bar.

"B-b-but aren't you my buddy?" I pleaded ironically. He didn't reply, but acted as though he had never seen me. So much for glad hands, good-time pals, and party buddies wherever they're found.

EDWARD HOYT

Court Day

If you walk to the corner, you get a pretty good view of Yankee Stadium. If you walk around the corner, you get a pretty good view of police and corrections officers hustling bodies to trials or bookings. 251 West 161 Street is the address of Bronx Criminal Court and Bronx Central Booking.

It's not what I expected a courthouse to be like. It looks like a Greek temple, except, instead of priests and crowds of the devout, there are various court officers hanging around for security, I guess, and police officers hanging out waiting for their cases to be called.

I went to courtroom AR 9. There was no problem getting in: all that was needed was a quick explanation of my intention and the court officer admitted me. The court I was in was called by Police Officer Michael Cody of the Bronx Task Force "a court for minor offenses."

This is not Perry Mason's or even "The People's" court. It's more like the dean's office. The first thing anyone would notice is the judge's bench, which is totally out of proportion with the rest of the room and its contents. Surrounding the bench are several regular-sized desks: to the right, the court officer's desk; to the left, the stenographer's; and in front, a long desk the only purpose of which I could discern being to keep people as far away as possible from his majesty.

There's no room for a large audience because of the size of the judge's bench. In all, about thirty people could fit in the room. I was sitting in the back as people filtered in. First, about ten uniformed patrolmen came in in succession; then, some fifteen civilians—the motley crew of defendants—came in piecemeal. Some of them seemed not to have a care in the world while others, especially a father whose son was caught stealing fireworks, were overwrought. Again, especially the father—he was concerned not only about his son but also about his lawyer, who was busy associating himself with the gypsy cab driver in front of me.

Here we all waited together. And we waited and waited and waited. Judge Felix—I learned his name from Court Officer O'Donnell—was the missing ingredient, the captain without whom the ship could not sail, the key without which the engine of the court could not run. He, we were informed, was in his chambers next to the courtroom, probably (I thought) on the phone making plans for his lunch.

Finally, we were graced with his presence. Everyone stood, Court Officer O'Donnell mumbled something out, and we were on our way. First off was a young man with a summons for drinking in public. The man pleaded guilty and the judge promptly gave him a $25.00 fine. The teenager with his dad and lawyer also pleaded guilty and got his fine reduced after a long-winded statement from the lawyer. A tall man who had been caught with an ounce of marijuana pleaded guilty with an explanation. After his explanation he was summarily fined $100.00. Fifteen minutes had gone by and the judge had not looked up once. For a minute I even thought that he might have dozed off. But he was awake all right, but punch drunk from the whole scenario. He didn't really listen; he just went through the motions by rote.

Judge Felix finally did look up and looked annoyed as well. The defendant who had been summoned to court for not having a motor vehicle tax sticker in his gypsy cab couldn't speak English. The judge motioned to the court officer and in a few minutes he returned with a short, neatly dressed Spanish woman. She was briefed on the situation and then the theatrics began. The judge, the defendant, and the Spanish woman began a web of discussion that was impossible to follow. And the whole thing proved to be much ado in any case. The cab driver produced the proper sticker and that was that: "Not Guilty." As to the woman, she stayed and translated for one more defendant, then went about her business, which I assumed was translating in one and then another courtroom. Later, my friend Cody told me that she is in fact a cleaning woman in the building.

All in all, it was a frustrating and disappointing experience. Many of the police I saw came to court poorly prepared—at best with notes they couldn't decipher half of the time—and spoke with as much authority as a bunch of ten-year-olds. The judge just seemed to be a sour grape. But what most turned me off was the motley crowd of defendants and their attitude toward the court and the system of justice it represents. If I had to face this bunch every day, I guess I'd turn sour too.

According to Police Officer Cody, upwards of fifty thousand cases come through this one building alone in a year. That is a staggering load for society, for the judicial system, and for that cleaning woman too.

WILLIAM O'CONNELL

The Hoyt essay is full of slang, which is not inappropriate to dialogue and here helps to create a casual tone that seems right for the subject matter (note how diction goes into the making of tone). Such phrases as "bail out," "stick around," "hit the street," and "smoke a spliff" lend color to the essay and a sense of authenticity. Thus, Hoyt's informal diction, which results in an informal style, works for him in getting us to accept his definition of "Party Buddies." Of course, this kind of style would not be appropriate to most writing. The kind of style that is appropriate is exemplified by the O'Connell paper. O'Connell's diction (as well, in fact, as his syntax) is what we've called "ordinary," the diction of ordinary good English. His is the middle style.

I want to plug this style. The informal style is not suited to most writing; the formal style, an example of which follows, too often does not produce good writing.

> One's vocational calling should reflect the multifaceted nature of one's personality. What one chooses as a vocation, that is, should be an extension of one's whole, or complete, self. Of course, to attain the fullness of a complete self takes calculated effort. Such completion can be achieved by the utilization of three personal "examinations," each of which is necessary to become one with oneself. These examinations—of one's emotions, outlook, and insight—allow one to deal with the external world, or with one's interactions with it. It is incumbent upon us to examine each in turn.

This was written by a student majoring in sociology, but it reads like a good deal of writing in various specialized fields. Perhaps—though I doubt it—such writing is appropriate in the context of a given discipline. But whether it is or not, it is not good writing whatever the rationale. Like most formal writing, its tone (note again how diction creates tone) is cold, aloof, and even pompous, and certainly the paragraph is unnecessarily difficult to understand. In any event, the formal style is no better suited to most writing occasions than is the informal style. If you are instructed to write in this style, then do; but know that what you write is unlikely to be good writing.

So the middle style is the style to emulate. Neither unduly chummy on the one hand nor overly reserved on the other, the middle style helps create the voice of a person seriously engaged in communicating to the reader, of a warm and friendly human being talking to other human beings. Outside of specialized fields, at least, this kind of voice carries real weight with readers. As to diction, the middle style calls for words that people ordinarily use in social situations in general—not slang for the most part and not a bunch of ten-dollar words, just the vocabulary that most people use most of the time. "It is incumbent upon" is formal; "C'mon" is slang; "Let's" is in the middle.

However, it is easy to be tempted away from good writing. Bad writing abounds not because most people aren't good writers but because in many quarters bad writing is the norm, what is expected, what is rewarded. I'm thinking specifically of what is called the "official style," which is a kind of formal style widely used by bureaucrats, administrators, insurance companies, and the like. It is a style in which nouns predominate over verbs, and *being* verbs (*is, are, will be*, and so forth) predominate over action verbs; big words are generally preferred to ordinary words; the passive voice predominates over the active; and sentence structure is generally contorted: prepositional phrases are strung together and frequently positioned between the subject and the verb of a sentence so that the reader entirely loses sight of what the subject is. This style has become so pervasive that it demands further attention.

Two Styles: A Contrast and Prescription

Here are two passages on exactly the same subject but in different styles. Which of the two do you find preferable? Why?

Official Style

In the next few minutes, it is my intention to do three things. First will be a description of the features of greatest salience of what is popularly called medicalese. Second will be a description of two consequences of that style. And third will be the presentation of one rule of great simplicity which if followed about 75 percent of the time would result in the transformation of medicalese into a prose of greater clarity, that merely happened to be about medicine. A further intention in the presentation of the following is the illustration of that greater clarity of style. You have in your hands another version of what I will read, a version expressly written for the illustration of the differences between the style in use in this speech and in a prose style of utter straightforwardness.

Ordinary Style

In the next few minutes, I intend to do three things. First I will describe the most salient feature of what is popularly called medicalese. Second, I will describe two consequences of that style. And third, I will present one very simple rule which if followed about 75 percent of the time would almost entirely transform medicalese into clear prose that merely happened to be about medicine. Furthermore, I intend to illustrate what I consider to be that clearer style in the way I present what follows. You have in your hands another version of what I will read, a version expressly written to differ from the style I am using now in the same way that medicalese differs from utterly straightforward prose.

The second paragraph, I hope, is the one you preferred stylistically. In fact, it is so much better than the first that the comparison is almost unfair. The first is static in effect, for *to be* is a verb of being, not of action. So the reader of the "official" example is subjected to "First will be a description" instead of the ordinary style's crisp "I will describe." The first passage just sits there like a lump. The second, with its action verbs, seems vibrant and alive. It is also far less wordy. Notice one more difference: the second passage contains ten prepositional phrases; the first contains fully twenty-five, most of which come in strings ("*of* the features *of* greatest salience *of* what is," "*in* the transformation *of* medicalese *into* a prose *of* greater clarity"). Not only do these strings make the passage stringy and wordy but they are also rhythmically monotonous, their monotony adding to the lumpishness of the passage.

The extensive use of noun phrases is another numbing feature of the official style. Nouns are piled on nouns in phrases like "the computer program assessment planning development effort" until we don't know whether we're coming or going. Related words like subjects and objects are characteristically separated, thus making this kind of writing all the harder to understand. And the extensive use of the passive voice is usually a mark of the official style. English has two voices, the active and the passive. The *active voice* expresses an action performed by the subject of the verb: "I performed the experiment." In the *passive voice*, some form of *to be* (*is, was, were*, and so forth) is placed before the past participle (a part of the verb usually ending in *-ed*) so that an action *done to* rather than *done by* is expressed: "The experiment *was performed.*" (In the preceding two sentences, the first sentence, about the active voice, is written in the active voice; the second, about the passive voice, uses only passive constructions.)

Note what a convenient way of avoiding responsibility the passive voice affords and what the features of officialese together serve to do: to keep the reader from understanding what is being said. For an example, all you need do is read an insurance policy. I have a Ph.D. in English, yet I can't make head or tail of any of my policies. Might it be that I'm not meant to understand? At any rate, here is a favorite sentence of mine in the official style and its translation:

Original

The notice that emanated from the department headed by you has been filed in the course of the work situation on the day previous to this for permanent disposition.

Translation

I threw your notice into the wastebasket yesterday.

Why would anyone want to write in such a way? One reason, no doubt, is that this bloated style makes some people feel important. Perhaps they also feel that it's more objective, more scientific. And anything that is scientific carries prestige in our society. But the main reason, I think, is that many people don't want to communicate; they want to obfuscate. Why? I'll use an anecdote for answer. I was in a country last summer where tips are usually—but not always—included in hotel and restaurant bills. Looking over the dessert menu of a well-known restaurant in this country, I was wondering whether I should tip or not when I saw the following notice at the bottom of the menu:

All prices inclusive of gratuities.

What would you have done? Like other Americans I spoke to later, I left a tip. But the sentence translates, "Tips included." Obfuscation pays.

However, if you're interested in writing prose that people can understand easily, then you will eliminate from your writing all of the devices of bureaucratic prose that we've examined. The next time you write an essay, do the following:

1. Circle all forms of the verb *to be*.

2. Circle all prepositional phrases.

3. Circle any words you don't really know or that can be replaced by a shorter word.

4. Circle all noun phrases.

5. Circle all related words (for instance, subject and verb) separated by more than a phrase or a short clause.

Then do as follows:

1. Of *to be* forms ask, "Who is doing what to whom?" If you're dealing with a passive construction and can answer the question, the chances are that you would be better off changing the construction to the active voice.

2. If you have more than two (and sometimes even two) prepositional phrases running together, find another construction.

3. Get rid of any word you know you don't really know, and substitute a shorter word for a longer whenever possible.

4. Restate any noun phrase of even more than two nouns and certainly more than three.

5. Don't separate related words if possible. And when you do separate related words, make sure that the separation will not cause confusion.

6. Finally, something that lovers of the official style have never done: read everything you write aloud with emphasis and feeling. If, indeed, what you've written can be so read, and if it sounds like English the way *you yourself* speak it, then there has to be something right about what you've written. If it is also coherent, then you have something worth putting your name on.

SYNTAX

Syntax refers to the positioning of single words and related groups of words (phrases and clauses) in sentences, to the relationship of position and meaning, and to the various ways a sentence can be structured. Because sentences are composed of words, diction is a prime constituent of style; because words can be arranged in different ways, syntax is the other prime constituent.

There are four sentence types:

simple	A simple sentence consists of a subject and a verb (*Mary threw up*), a complement if necessary (Mary threw the *ball*), and any modifiers (Mary threw *the* ball *to Harry at third*). Both subject and verb may be compounds (*Mary and Harry* also *jumped and danced* for joy).
compound	A compound sentence consists of two simple sentences (called independent clauses) joined by one of the seven coordinating conjunctions—*and, but, for, or, nor, yet, so*. (Mary threw the ball to Harry at third, *and* Harry tagged the runner out.)
complex	A complex sentence consists of an independent clause and one or more dependent clauses, a dependent clause being a clause that is headed by a subordinating conjunction like *because, although, until* or a relative pronoun like *who, that, which* and that would be an independent sentence or clause if not so headed. (Mary threw the ball to Harry at third *because she knew enough to make a safety play.*)
compound-complex	A compound-complex sentence consists of two or more independent clauses and one or more dependent clauses. (Mary threw the ball to Harry at third *because* she knew enough to make a safety play, *and* Harry, *although* he is usually a klutz, caught the ball and tagged the runner out at third.)

That's it—four sentence types to choose from. But the style of one's writing can depend in large measure upon the choice. Hemingway's famous style, for instance, is based on his use of simple sentences, which in concentration create a sense of spareness and a rugged, down-to-earth voice:

It was now lunch time and they were all sitting under the double green fly of the dining tent pretending that nothing had happened.

"Will you have lime juice or lemon squash?" Macomber asked.

"I'll have a gimlet," Robert Wilson told him.

"I'll have a gimlet too. I need something," Macomber's wife said.

"I suppose it's the thing to do," Macomber agreed. "Tell him to make three gimlets."

William Faulkner's style, in contrast, is one of highly complex and often involuted sentences, a style fit to give voice to a similarly complex state of mind.

From a little after two o'clock until almost sundown of the long still hot weary dead September afternoon they sat in what Miss Cold-field still called the office because her father had called it that—a dim hot airless room with the blinds all closed and fastened for forty-three summers because when she was a girl someone had believed that light and moving air carried heat and that dark was always cooler, and which (as the sun shone fuller and fuller on that side of the house) became latticed with yellow slashes full of dust motes which Quentin thought of as being flecks of the dead old dried paint itself blown inward from the scaling blinds as wind might have blown them.

A characteristic syntax, then, gives rise to a particular kind of style, which, in turn, engenders a particular kind of sensibility.

Another aspect of syntax intimately linked to style is the patterning of sentences. Four ways of patterning in particular demand attention.

Loose Syntax

Loose syntax is the typical syntax of our language. We are an impetu-ous lot, spilling the beans with our first words. That is, we speakers of English tend to blurt out our main information up front and to put modification, qualification, reasons, or whatever second. So, typically, we would say:

I killed my wife because I hated her.

I feel down every spring for some reason I don't understand.

A whole passage composed of such sentences, especially if they are simple, will affect the reader with a sense of plain-spokenness, urgency, or humdrumness depending on such other factors as diction and context. But whatever the effect may be, it will result from the choices the writer has made and consequently from the style of the given piece of writing. Style and effect, finally, are one.

Periodic Syntax

Periodic syntax is the opposite of loose syntax; the main information of a periodic sentence comes at the end. Periodic syntax is especially well suited to building to a climax and thereby placing special emphasis on the element that comes last in a sentence. In this regard, contrast the examples of loose syntax with the following examples of periodic syntax:

Because I hated my wife, *I killed her.*

Every spring, for some reason I don't understand, *I feel down.*

These statements are much more dramatic than the equivalent statements in loose syntax. Of course, one wouldn't want every statement to be dramatic. Thus, periodic syntax is a variant rather than the norm. Loose syntax provides our norm; periodic syntax should be thought of as a possible variant to be used when the sense of drama is appropriate. The following example, which you might recast into loose syntax and compare as to effect with the original, is periodic. Note the drama the structure of the sentence lends to the statement, which clearly builds to a climax with its strategically placed last clause:

If life seems tedious, if liberty becomes just another word, if happiness means nothing but egotistical gratification, *then our constitution will be worth nothing more than the paper it is written on.*

The stylist uses periodic syntax to vary the sentence structure of a passage (we'll return to the subject of sentence variety shortly) and to gain emphasis. The last sample sentence, for instance, causes a degree of suspense and so gains emphasis with its resolution. All this is achieved through syntax alone, without the reader's necessarily being conscious of how. So, if you want to gain emphasis quietly, subtly, but surely, use periodic syntax, especially to structure key sentences containing your main ideas.

Parallel Syntax

Parallelism results from putting similar items into similar grammatical constructions. Here are some examples, the first of which in each case is faulty and the second correct.

1. For Christmas I want a *bike*, a *Ping-Pong table*, and *to get new skates*. (noun, noun, and infinitive phrase)
   For Christmas I want a *bike*, a *Ping-Pong table*, and new *skates*. (noun, noun, and noun)

2. The college reports a *growth* in students admitted but *that costs have grown even more rapidly*. (noun and subordinate clause)
   The college reports a *growth* in students admitted but an even more rapid *growth* in costs. (noun and noun)

3. *To be* or perhaps *I should kill myself*. (infinitive and independent clause)
   To be or not *to be*. (infinitive and infinitive)

Compared or contrasted items as well as correlative construction also call for parallel syntax. Here are some examples, the first of which in each case again is faulty and the second correct:

1. *Fiction* no longer interests me as much as *to read nonfiction*. (noun and infinitive phrase)
   Fiction no longer interests me as much as *nonfiction*. (noun and noun)

2. Her diamond is said to be valuable as much for its *luster* as *because it is big*. (prepositional phrase and subordinate clause)
   Her diamond is said to be valuable as much for its *luster* as for its *size*. (noun and noun)

3. The coach told the team both *to buckle up* and *they should buckle down*. (infinitive and independent clause)
   The coach told the team both *to buckle up* and *to buckle down*. (infinitive and infinitive)

4. The head of the bank was thought to be not only *capable* but also a *person* of honor. (adjective and noun)

The head of the bank was thought to be not only *capable* but also *honorable.* (adjective and adjective)

Over and above grammatical considerations, parallelism is a fine stylistic tool that can have a number of rhetorical effects. Here are four sentences marked by parallel syntax. How does each affect you?

I came, I saw, I conquered.

A man should speak Spanish to his god, French to his mistress, but German to his horse.

Which would you prefer: to read a novel by Henry James or to be crushed to death by weights?

When one is young, one reads Hemingway; when one is old, one reads hardly at all.

Caesar's famous sentence (the first sentence in the preceding list) conveys a sense of mastery; here is a person in complete control of things. But, you might say, "That's what the words mean. What does syntax have to do with it?" My answer is break the parallelism and see: "I came; I saw; and conquering was what I achieved." The emphasis and sense of dominance imparted by Caesar's parallelism are completely lost in the revision, which sounds more like the utterance of a bureaucrat than of a conqueror. The parallelism, along with the anticlimactic arrangement of its parallel elements, makes the second sentence satirically humorous in effect. Also humorous, the third sentence defines by way of its parallel infinitive phrases, which form a kind of syntactical equation. Finally, in its balancing of young and old, a balancing achieved by parallel syntax, the last sentence has about it a sense of inevitability and very much a sense of pathos. That these effects are created primarily by the syntax of the sentence is demonstrated by the following revision, curt and bloodless: One reads Hemingway when young; old people hardly read at all.

But it's impossible to demonstrate the full range of parallel syntax in discrete sentences alone. For good writers not only put together individual sentences that are parallel in structure but they also put together two or more sentences that run parallel—and even whole paragraphs. Abraham Lincoln's "Gettysburg Address" shows how parallelism can inform a whole composition:

Four score and seven years ago our fathers brought forth on this continent, a new nation, conceived in Liberty, and dedicated to the proposition that all men are created equal. Now we are engaged in a great civil war, testing whether that nation or any nation so conceived and so dedicated, can long endure. We are met on a great battlefield of that war. We have come to dedicate a portion of that field, as a final resting place for those who here gave their lives that that nation might live. It is altogether fitting and proper that we should do this. But, in a larger sense, we can not dedicate—we can not consecrate—we can not hallow—this ground. The brave men, living and dead, who struggled here have consecrated it, far above our poor power to add or detract. The world will little note, nor long remember what we say here, but it can never forget what they did here. It is for us the living, rather, to be dedicated here to the unfinished work which they who fought here have thus far so nobly advanced. It is rather for us to be here dedicated to the great task remaining before us—that from these honored dead we take increased devotion to that cause for which they gave the last full measure of devotion—that we here highly resolve that these dead shall not have died in vain—that this nation, under God, shall have a new birth of freedom—and that government of the people, by the people, for the people, shall not perish from the earth.

Standard in its diction and straightforward in its syntax, the address has a tone of earnestness and the voice of sincerity. Pomposity and self-aggrandizement are precluded by Lincoln's diction and phrasing. Further, the very simplicity lends a stateliness to the utterance as it moves quietly yet emphatically from point to point. The voice of Lincoln's speech is that of a simple man roused to passionate conviction by the gravity of the moment. We would be wrong, however, to think of Lincoln's address as just the spontaneous outpouring of a simple man speaking from the heart, with no thought of matters of rhetoric and style. Lincoln's artistry is demonstrated by his parallelism. The address contains a number of instances of parallel construction, two of which are especially striking: "we can not dedicate—we can not consecrate—we can not hallow" and "of the people, by the people, for the people." Stylistically, parallelism lends emphasis as well as a sense of sureness to the voice of a piece of writing. It also creates a rhythm of balance—prose rhythm being mainly an offshoot of syntax—and suggests, thereby, a balanced, reasoning mind at work.

These are very much the effects of Lincoln's address. Then, too, parallel phrases and sentences, and sometimes even paragraphs, are often memorable because of their parallelism, as Lincoln's "government of the people, by the people, for the people" has proved to be.

Clearly, Lincoln was a master of words and verbal patterns. He is rightly considered a great prose stylist, one who could control the element of style and make it serve his purposes. There is no way of putting words together that will not exhibit style of some sort—whether mature or childish, arresting or vapid, lively or dull. The trick is to control style, to choose words and to put them together deliberately to create the tone and voice best suited to your purpose.

Balanced Syntax

Finally, there is balanced syntax, a special kind of parallelism that sets parallel elements in opposition. All of the following sentences are syntactically balanced:

You go your way and I'll go mine.

I come to bury Caesar, not to praise him.

His intelligence tests suggest that he could do well; his achievement scores suggest that he won't.

To be French is to be like no one else; to be American is to be like everyone else.

Each of these sentences moves easily on, creating a sense of balance through parallelism. But now that sense goes to underscore discordant elements, similarity serving to highlight dissimilarity. Such is another use of parallel construction.

SENTENCE VARIETY

The ancient Chinese had a torture that doesn't seem too terrible at first sight—just a feather stroking an arm. But the torture was guaranteed to drive anyone mad if prolonged. Some writing resembles this torture in the sameness of its sentences. One simple sentence follows another and another and another until the reader finds the monotony intolerable. The stylistic principle to be gleaned here is that sentences should vary in length and kind.

Avoid using many syntactically similar sentences in a row except for special effect. Likewise, avoid using a word or phrase over and over in close proximity. For instance, the following sentences, each of which begins with a participial phrase, are fine individually, but together they are irksome:

> Realizing that he would be late if he didn't hurry, Harry ran for the bus. Fearing a heart attack, however, he slowed down. Seeing the bus a long way off, he relaxed. Arriving at the stop, he stood and waited.

And deeing da dee, he deed and dawed. And so on, and so on, and so on. The structural repetition establishes a rhythm that very quickly becomes tedious. Think of your poor reader and remember the Chinese feather torture.

As far as I'm concerned, the golden rule of writing sentences is this: *As short as possible with clarity.* But how does this rule tally with the principle just stated about varying sentence length and kind? Aren't simple sentences short and clear? Why not, therefore, write only in simple sentences if "as short as possible with clarity" is the rule? Well, aside from the monotony of a string of simple sentences, such a string generally produces a passage that is incoherent. That is, although each of the sentences of a passage may be clear in and of itself, the passage they constitute may nevertheless be muddy or entirely opaque because the relationship of its sentences is not clear. Look again at two paragraphs we considered earlier when we took up the subject of coherence. The first is composed all of simple sentences, which do not cohere; the revision attains both coherence and variety, chiefly by subordination.

> We studied the poem "The Road Not Taken" in high school. Robert Frost is known as having been an individualist. That's what my teacher said the poem is about. You have to go away from the beaten path and make a path of your own. I thought it was okay. What my teacher said seemed okay. I liked the last two lines. We studied the poem in college. It means something else. The poem concerns the difficulty of making important choices. Often there's nothing much to go on.

> When we studied Robert Frost's poem "The Road Not Taken" in high school, we were told that Frost was a "rugged individualist"

whose poem concerns individualism, or going away from the beaten path and making a path of one's own. That interpretation seemed good to me at the time because in the last line the poet says right out, "I took the one less traveled by." Now, however, I believe the poem is about something else. Having studied it again in college, I think that Frost is getting at the difficulty of making important choices when there's nothing much to go on.

The short simple sentence, especially when saved for some key point, can be effective. But strings of short simple sentences should be avoided except for special effect. They result in writing that is choppy and usually incoherent as well. Strings of compound sentences are no better. They produce a "stringy" style that tends to sound childish:

> Our committee voted for student parking on campus, *and so* students will be able to park near their classes, *and* that should make things easier on all of us, *and so* we should all be pleased by the outcome.

That sounds like a child reporting on the day's events: "We went to the zoo and saw the elephants and then we fed the monkeys and had a chocolate ice-cream cone," and so on. Among other things, style reflects maturity. The stringy style is childish; the mature mind differentiates and subordinates.

Repositioning and Substitution

Also, like strings of short simple sentences, the stringy style is monotonous and boring. The careful writer always revises with variety in mind. Subordination, as we've seen, is one way of gaining variety. Varying sentence length—with short sentences used, for instance, to punctuate a point analyzed in longer sentences—is also a way of gaining variety, as is varying sentence type (simple, compound, complex, compound-complex). Then, too, some sentences should be loose, some periodic; some should be parallel, some balanced. Variation can also be achieved simply by repositioning elements within a sentence or substituting one kind of element for another. Here are some examples:

Repositioning

1. John was a whiz in class.
   In class, John was a whiz.

2. Wanda worked after school to earn money for college.
   To earn money for college, Wanda worked after school.

3. The balloon man let go of his balloons because of the wind.
   Because of the wind, the balloon man let go of his balloons.

4. Having been struck by lightning, the old tree split in half.
   The old tree, having been struck by lightning, split in half.

Substitution

1. The movie was long and boring, and so it put me to sleep.
   Long and boring, the movie put me to sleep.

2. We went for a drive and saw the woods, liking what we saw.
   We drove through the woods and liked what we saw.

3. Charleston is a favorite city of mine, and I would like to live there someday.
   Someday I would like to live in Charleston, a favorite city of mine.
   Charleston, a favorite city of mine, is a place I'd like to live in someday.

4. Just a minute before she was to go on stage, Lily Langhorn died of a heart attack.
   Lily Langhorn died of a heart attack just as she was about to go on stage.
   About to go on stage, Lily Langhorn died of a heart attack.

Almost any sentence can be rephrased in various ways. Which should you choose and why? Clarity should be the primary consideration. Then length: a shorter sentence is usually preferable to a longer one if both say about the same thing. The sound and rhythm of each sentence should also be taken into account. Read everything you write aloud and ask of every sentence, "Would I ever say this?" If not, revise! Then, too, irrational factors come into play. You might just like one way of putting something better than another, though you don't know why. Your gut feeling is often a good guide. Finally, variety should always be a consideration. In choosing one construction or another, the writer should ask, "Is there a similar construction in other sentences in this passage?" If so, the criterion of choice is sentence variety, which is criterion enough.

Special Effects

However, although variety should usually be the rule, sometimes what I've called "special effects" can be an exception. Certain kinds of rhythm, resulting from the concentration of one or another type of sentence structure, can themselves communicate meaning. In their pronounced rhythmic dissimilarity, the following passages should illustrate this:

> As individuals we must join others. No time to quibble about survival being "a white issue." No time to claim you don't live here, too. Massive demonstrations are vital. Massive civil disobedience. And, in fact, massive anything that's necessary to save our lives.
>
> Talk with your family; organize your friends. Educate anybody you can get your mouth on. Raise money. Support those who go to jail.

> Moths that fly by day are not properly to be called moths; they do not excite that pleasant sense of dark autumn nights and ivy-blossom which the commonest yellow-underwing asleep in the shadow of the curtain never fails to rouse in us. They are hybrid creatures, neither gay like butterflies nor somber like their own species. Nevertheless the present specimen, with his narrow hay-colored wings, fringed with a tassel of the same color, seemed to be content with life.

Composed of very short simple sentences, the first passage (from Alice Walker's "Nuclear Madness, What You Can Do") is sharp and insistent in its rhythm, which imparts a sense of urgency apt for the subject matter. In contrast, the second passage (from Virginia Woolf's "The Death of the Moth") is slow and graceful in its forward motion. The mind here is at ease, peaceful and in a state of self-reflexive meditation. Both reflect what style means in connection with the best writing: style is the writer's means of communicating not just sense but sensibility as well.

Paring Down

I never fail to shock my students when they get back their first papers and discover that I have penciled out from a third to a half of their words. The fat content is enormous, and it's all saturated. An equivalent amount of cholesterol in the bloodstream would kill anyone. And such excess, metaphorically speaking, is much more than enough to kill a piece of prose. But beginning writers aren't to blame. Usually all their experience has taught them that verbiage is a virtue—from the 500-word theme (usually padded out with unnecessary words), to every form they've had to fill out, to communiqués from the school principal. The more words and the bigger, the better—that's what the message seems to be. Well, believe me, when it comes to good writing, less is more. As short as possible with clarity—that remains my rule.

So when a phrase will do instead of a clause, use a phrase; and when a word will do just as well, use a single word. Reduce whenever possible. For instance:

I killed a bird that had yellow feathers. → I killed a bird with yellow feathers. → I killed a yellow bird.

We move here from eight to seven to five words. Is there any difference in meaning? No, so five words should be used instead of eight. Now consider the two passages that follow, one almost twice as long as the other. Which do you think is easier to read, is greater in impact, and, simply, is more fun?

In New York City there are three kinds of people who each contribute something different to the atmosphere. I will first describe these three kinds of people and then relate how they affect my perception of the city. First, there is the commuter, who prefers to live outside the city, coming in only to work. Second, there are the natives, who were born there and more or less take everything about the place for granted. Finally, there are those who were born somewhere else and have moved to New York City. The first kind makes the city seem jumpy (because they are always coming and going). The second kind makes the city seem very old and ordinary and settled because they've been there forever and are pretty settled. The third kind is here because they think the city will be the answer to their dreams. After all, they left their native homes to come here. Sometimes they are disappointed and sometimes not, but they usually attribute these feelings to the city, and that makes the city seem more or less exciting. They also give more to the city artswise and businesswise than the commuters who come to New York only to work and the natives who just take everything for granted.

There are roughly three New Yorks. There is, first, the New York of the man or woman who was born here, who takes the city for granted and accepts its turbulence as natural and inevitable. Second, there is the New York of the commuter—the city that is devoured by locusts each day and spat out each night. Third, there is the New York of the person who was born somewhere else and came to New York in quest of something. Of these three trembling cities the greatest is the last—the city of final destination, the city that is a goal. It is this third city that accounts for New York's high-strung disposition, its poetical deportment, its dedication to the arts, and its incomparable achievements. Commuters give the city its tidal restlessness, natives give it solidity and continuity, but the settlers give it passion.

Why should anyone want to read the first passage when the second (by E. B. White) is possible? Life is short. Pare down.

Take adjectives. Don't clog your writing with them. A few go a long way. And always ask of your adjectives, is there any other kind? "The destructive damage caused by the storm was awesome." Is there any other kind of damage? When it comes to adjectives, be a contrarian. Use an adjective only when you are making a real distinction. And when it is possible to use a verb alone instead of a verb and an adverb, do so. For instance,

He walked unsteadily. → He staggered.

Watch, too, for sentences that can be read in more than one way and revise to eliminate the unwanted reading:

The two men were determined to have a blood alcohol level of .15 percent.

I can see them now, chug-a-lugging and chanting, ".15 percent or bust." Here, "determined to have" should be changed to "found to have."

Also, of course, know what your words mean. "All by herself she plays solo"—which I heard an announcer say on the radio the other day in introducing a solo performance—is absurd. Solo means "alone." "She plays solo" is what was meant—a saving of three words, or 50 percent.

"Also, of course, know what your words mean." I glibly say "of course," but what writer has never used words that he or she doesn't really know, big words, fancy words, but empty words with no precise meaning in the context? Don't! Such words merely add to the fat content. Contrast the following sentences:

> Illumination is required to be extinguished upon vacating the premises.

> Shut off the lights when you leave the room.

Although the second sentence is only one word shorter than the first, it is fully fourteen syllables shorter (and also in the active voice). A plain-spoken diction, like that of the second sentence, is always more concise than the posturing diction of the first.

As well as leading to greater conciseness and promoting a tone that sounds like an actual human being, paring down can solve a host of specific problems. For example, take this terribly wordy sentence:

> Mark likes football, and baseball is also a sport that he likes.

Not only is this sentence wordy but it is also awkward. Subjects, like verb tense and voice, should not be shifted unnecessarily like this. Paring down solves both problems at once:

> Mark likes both football and baseball.

The second sentence is preferable to the first on every score.

When Not to Pare

The writer must learn what words to delete. By the same token, the writer must come to understand when words cannot be deleted. In parallel constructions, for instance, certain words should be repeated if there is any chance of confusion. The next two sentences exemplify when a word in a parallel construction may be deleted and when the word must be left in.

> Ellen wanted me to meet her, (*to*) get her bags, and (*to*) drive her home.
> [The second and third *to* may be deleted here.]

> On the passage over, many pilgrims began *to* fear that they wouldn't make it and *to* make their peace accordingly.

[Here, the repetition of *to* is essential so that the reader knows immediately that *to fear* and *to make* are the parallel elements and not *make* and *make*.]

That, also, may frequently be omitted, but sometimes the omission would be confusing and so the word must be used. Consider the next sentence in this regard.

Martin observed the passerby in the raincoat had dropped his wallet.

Here, *that* is necessary to eliminate the possible initial (and confusing) meaning, "Martin observed the passerby":

Martin observed *that* the passerby in the raincoat had dropped his wallet.

Another situation where paring can get you into difficulty involves pairs of verbs that take different prepositions. For instance, *contribute* takes *to*, whereas *detract* takes *from*. Therefore, the following sentence needs an extra word:

These criticisms neither contribute nor detract from the value of the book.

For the sake of both usage and sense, *to* must be supplied:

These criticisms neither contribute to nor detract from the value of the book.

A similar situation occurs with shifts of tense with compound verbs. For instance, if using a compound construction involving a shift from the past to the present (or future), you would have to express both tenses:

Incorrect:

Gale has never and cannot be truly open with anyone.

Revised:

Gale has never *been* and cannot be truly open with anyone.

Comparisons also sometimes require an extra word or two. Try to supply the word or words needed to complete the following comparisons.

Broken glass around a pool is more dangerous than a picnic table.

Snow in Miami is as scarce as the desert.

Sometimes advisors aid a patient's family more than the patient.

Capone runs faster than any member on her team.

Marcos invested in New York real estate, gems, and paintings.

Is a picnic table dangerous? Is the desert scarce? Does a patient try to aid his or her family? And can someone run faster than everyone on a team, herself included? Are there in fact gems and paintings that come only from New York? These sentences are not logical as they stand. But only a word or two (or three at the most) will make each fully logical. Contrast the preceding sample sentences and the following revisions:

Broken glass around the pool is more dangerous than *around* a picnic table.

Snow in Miami is as scarce as *it is in* the desert.

Sometimes advisors aid a patient's family more than *they do* the patient.

Capone runs faster than any *other* member on the team.

Marcos invested in New York real estate, in gems, and in paintings.

[Or better yet:]
Marcos invested in gems, paintings, and New York real estate.

In sum, as a writer you have to become sensitive to what can and what can't be cut. Usually, many words can and so should be struck out because they don't add anything and may even detract from clarity and grace. However, one or two extra words are sometimes needed for the sake of logic and clarity. These you must supply.

CHANGING CONSTRUCTIONS

Sitting down to order a shipment of animals from Australia, a zoo-keeper wrote:

> Please send me an emu, three ostriches, three koalas, and two platy-
> puses.

He paused. "Platypuses? Platypi?" he mused. He couldn't make up his mind. So he wrote:

> Please send me an emu, three ostriches, three koalas, and a platypus.
> While you're at it, send me another platypus.

The moral of this story is *when in doubt, change the construction.*

Indeed, like paring down, changing a construction can often solve a problem instantly. For example, it's always possible to get around a problem with tense by simply applying the platypus principle. You write, "I wanted to work in a place where there *was?/is?* a good working atmosphere." You can't decide which tense to use and you don't much like either solution. Why not avoid tense entirely and simply use a prepositional phrase: "I wanted to work in a place with a good working atmosphere." Or you write, "I knew her. Her name *was* Rosy." But that sounds as though she's dead. Maybe she is, but you don't know that she is for a fact. What to do? Well, you could say, "I knew her. Her name was, and probably still is, Rosy." But that's terribly awkward. What about, "I knew her. She liked to be called Rosy." That would do if factual. But perhaps the best solution would be simply "I knew Rosy." These last examples suggest that changing constructions and paring down tend to go together. And so they do. Problems always result from the use of constructions that are too complex for the purpose at hand. Simplify, simplify! Begin by simplifying the next sentence:

> Whether I am reading the paper tonight or ten years ago, I always
> turn to Ann Landers first.

I am reading ten years ago? Ten years ago, I always turn? The problem could be solved by adding more words:

> Whether I am reading or was reading . . . , I always turn or turned. . . .

But that's awful. Simplify! The sentence can be saved by changing one word (and thus the construction) and cutting out seven other words:

> When reading the paper, I always turn to Ann Landers first.

The next and last sample sentence is correct technically but ungainly:

> Instead of confining himself or herself to a corner, a person should go out and meet people.

Say "confining himself or herself to" out loud. It's exhausting. Moreover, I doubt that anyone would ever speak like that. Listen to yourself as you write, and simplify.

> Instead of remaining in a corner, a person should go out and meet people.

Writing often entails avoiding problems by cutting or by changing constructions. And there are almost always other constructions that will do. The trick is not to become wedded to a given construction but, like the zookeeper, to order "another" platypus instead of platypuses or platypi.

EXERCISES

1. All of the following have to do with diction. Read each carefully and then answer any questions asked or do as instructed if an instruction is given.

    a. Characterize the diction of each of the following: informal, formal, or ordinary?
    (1) Boy, I'm bushed.
    (2) I'm really quite tired.
    (3) Fatigue has overcome me.

    b. The following might be how a student reports to friends an unpleasant conversation with a teacher. How would the student say the same thing to the dean of the school?

    > Yeah, the jerk said that any kids cutting more than six classes would get kicked out on their butts.

    c. Here are the last two lines of a poem by Anne Sexton entitled "To a Friend Whose Work Has Come to Triumph."

    > See him acclaiming the sun and come plunging down
    > While his sensible daddy goes straight into town.

    Judging from Sexton's diction alone, what do you think is her attitude toward "him" and what toward his father?

d. Here are five more lines from a poem—Josephine Miles's "Reason"—that has four speakers and concerns a man's unwillingness to move his car. What does the diction here tell about each of the four speakers?

> Said, Pull her up a bit, Mac, I want to unload there.
> Said, Pull her up my rear end, first come first serve.
> Said, Give her the gun, Bud, he needs a taste of his own bumper.
> Then the usher came out and got into the act:
> Said, pull her up, pull her up a bit, we need this space, sir.

e. Here is a passage from a satirical essay by Russell Baker entitled "Little Red Riding Hood Revisited." Characterize its diction. With regard to diction, what is being satirized?

> Once upon a point in time, a small person named Little Red Riding Hood initiated plans for the preparation, delivery, and transportation of foodstuffs to her grandmother, a senior citizen residing at a place of residence in a forest of indeterminate dimension.

2. The following sentences are in the "official" (bureaucratic) style. Restate each as concisely as you can in an ordinary style.

a. It is thought that a country with a noncommunistic orientation should be included in any decision-making process of international character entered into on the part of the government of the United States.

b. The recommendation decided upon by the committee must be weighed with deliberation in that, if this recommendation is to be implemented, the cost-factor will be high.

c. It should be understood that the recent actions taken by the command of NATO are a reflection of the mutual consent situation established by the original participants in the charter formation process.

d. Answers to these questions of some moment and gravity are being sought at the moment by the administration at every level through the academic program review process.

e. The administration is certainly concerned with the Transfer-Student problem, or, to put it another way, inter-institutional curricular coherence is a concern on our parts.

f. It is to be hoped that the meeting will be held in December at the Hilton Hotel in downtown Houston at or around 3 p.m. sponsored by this organization and thought to be a necessitated process orientation program.

g. The members of the board, or at least seven of the eight, whose consent was shown by a hand elevation process after a vocal demonstration favoring the motion, are by and large in agreement with the proposals of the president of the company.

3. Recast each of the following sentences, putting those in loose syntax into periodic syntax and those in periodic syntax into loose. How do the recast sentences differ in effect from the sentences as given? Which sentences are better in loose syntax and which in periodic? Why?

   a. Since rain is predicted for tomorrow, bring your umbrellas.

   b. I have a terrible craving for onions, though why I should I can't imagine.

   c. Don't take one more step if you value your life.

   d. Let's hope that conditions will improve in the fall, when the new shipment arrives.

   e. If I try a little harder, couldn't we work things out?

   f. I wonder why, since Harrison was defeated last time, he ran again.

   g. "Never," Helen declaimed, "not even for a moment, will I talk to that man again!"

   h. People get angry, it seems to me, when they feel insecure.

   i. Down by the seaside, where the good life is, is where I long to be.

   j. Provoking his teachers and fighting with all of his classmates, Guy is a problem child.

4. The following passage from Frederick Douglass's *Narrative of the Life of Frederick Douglass* is full of parallel constructions. Pick them out and be ready to discuss their effect in the passage as a whole.

   > [Mr. Gore, the overseer . . .] He was just proud enough to demand the most debasing homage of the slave, and quite servile enough to crouch, himself, at the feet of the master. He was ambitious enough to be contented with nothing short of the highest rank of overseers, and persevering enough to reach the height of his ambition. He was cruel enough to inflict the severest punishment, artful enough to descend to the lowest trickery, and obdurate enough to be insensible to the voice of a reproving conscience. He was, of all the overseers, the most dreaded by the

slaves. His presence was painful; his eye flashed confusion; and seldom was his sharp, shrill voice heard, without producing horror and trembling in their ranks.

Mr. Gore was a grave man, and, though a young man, he indulged in no jokes, said no funny words, seldom smiled. His words were in perfect keeping with his looks, and his looks were in perfect keeping with his words. Overseers will sometimes indulge in a witty word, even with the slaves; not so with Mr. Gore. He spoke but to command, and commanded but to be obeyed; he dealt sparingly with his words, and bountifully with his whip, never using the former where the latter would answer as well. When he whipped, he seemed to do so from a sense of duty, and feared no consequences. He did nothing reluctantly, no matter how disagreeable; always at his post, never inconsistent. He never promised but to fulfil. He was, in a word, a man of the most inflexible firmness and stone-like coolness.

5. For the sake of variety, rewrite each of the following according to the instruction(s) given.

a. Recast into a complex sentence:

On Saturday we saw *King Kong*. It is in black and white. It is still exciting.

b. Reposition the prepositional phrase in the second sentence:

She is a superb accountant on the job. She is an ace player on the court.

c. Make this a simple sentence opening with a prepositional phrase and closing with a participial phrase:

We took a trip to the zoo and saw the elephants and they ate peanuts.

d. Vary by repositioning the second phrase in the second sentence:

The human brain, an incredibly effective organ, contains millions of neurons. The average computer, a much less efficient machine, contains only a few thousand circuits.

e. Combine into a periodic sentence:

The boat left at nine. Molly missed it. She got up at ten.

f. Vary by repositioning one or another construction:

The boat rocked easily as the sun set. The crew sat fearfully as the captain came on deck.

g. Vary by substituting one construction for another:

The teacher fretted as the class turned taciturn. The teacher felt that the class had been lost and so fell into a state of despair.

h. Revise the following paragraph for variety and coherence. Remember that sometimes both can be gained by repositioning, sometimes by combining sentences by subordinating one to another, and sometimes by varying sentence types (both grammatical and rhetorical) as well as sentence lengths.

> Americans value their freedom. They appreciate their God-given right to own what they own. They appreciate their right to do what they want to do. They appreciate their right to do and to dream what they want. Americans dream many dreams. Their dreams shape the nation as a whole. America is the land of its people's dreams.

6.   The sentences that follow are all wordy, and some are problematic for other reasons as well. Correct both the wordiness and the problems by paring these sentences down. Do not, however, cut out any words needed to complete a construction and to make it make sense.

a. In the early to middle part of the month of September, strong winds called "hurricanes" form themselves in the Caribbean and often do a great deal of destructive damage both to the islands and to the coast of the United States.

b. In this modern world of ours today, people are constantly bombarded all day long with commercials trying to sell them something.

c. Not only did the students feel delighted feelings at the news that "The Walking Dead" was coming to the campus but they also realized that the group's well-known fame would be definitely good publicity for the college, bringing it positive notice.

d. After Cauldwell added up the figures, an error was discovered by him.

e. Angel threw the tiny, little round ball bearings further than did any other child in the class.

f. Nobody knows what a person does when you are all alone by yourself.

g. Commuters who go back and forth to work often get tired of it after they have done it for awhile or a certain period of time.

h. As to or as far as racism is concerned, it seems to me that blacks can be as guilty of it as whites can be.

i. Reynard was so entirely and absolutely certain that Melissa had sneakily stolen his book that he accused her of having done so in front of and to the principal.

j. No one should ask for or listen to the unwarranted advice from a person whom is unknown to them.

7. The sentences in this last block are somewhat wordy and/or monotonous, and some of their constructions are problematic. Remembering the platypus principle, revise these sentences by finding shorter or more varied ways of putting things.

a. At this point in time, my children have the capability of doing most of the chores.

b. The lead actress spoke in a low and hard-to-hear voice throughout the play.

c. The audience, which had become angry, booed the actress, who was blushing.

d. Joanne, who is my nitwit cousin, went ten years ago and still goes to an exercise parlor, where she does exercises.

e. The pedestrians raised their heads at the sound of the explosion, which was ear-shattering.

f. The head of the school board has resigned. The mayor has expressed regret at the resignation and the mayor said that Dr. Frankle will be missed.

g. The neighborhood, which was all but deserted, was scary when darkness came on.

h. In the event that you're late, expect to hear complaints on the part of my roommate.

i. The buildings along the primary roads across the United States all look alike. The shopping centers are all alike in size and seem to come from the same architectural mold. The malls also look alike whether they are in Maine or Oregon. The fast-food restaurants are all alike and this is the most obvious example of all.

j. Our bowling team, which was and is the best in the league, remains the best year after year.

A Short Glossary of Usage

The way we collectively use our common tongue determines both what and how words mean. *Collectively* is the operative word. The way I as a single individual use the language does not affect its shape nor does the way you use it nor do the earnest wishes of grammarians (some of whom have always tried to impose their views on the linguistic practices of the majority and have always failed). A common inheritance, our native tongue is common property, and we each must use it in light of this fact. Every writer, especially, must develop a strong sense of contemporary usage with regard to grammar and syntax, the meanings of words, idiomatic constructions and meanings, spelling, levels of diction, and so forth. What follows is a compilation of words and phrases frequently used incorrectly (according to contemporary usage) by beginning writers. Read over these entries and mark any that you need to learn. Then come back and learn them.

accept, except *Accept* is a verb meaning *to receive;* as a verb, *except* means "to take issue with," and as a preposition it means "excluding." For example,

I *accept* the honor you bestow on me.

We must *except* what Roberts says about the company.

I got good grades in every subject *except* astronomy.

affect, effect A verb, *affect* means *to have an impact on.* Usually a noun, *effect* means *the result of an action.* So one could affect an effect. *Effect* can also be a verb meaning *to bring about.* So a writer might be said to *effect* a resolution that *affects* the reader in such a way that the *effect* of the story is happy. But *effect* is not frequently used as a verb. Thus, if you remember that *affect* is a verb and that *effect* is usually a noun, this pair should not cause you much trouble.

aggravate The word means *to intensify an annoyance* and not just *to annoy* or *irritate*. Thus, one might say, "You *aggravated* my headache" but not "You *aggravate* me." *Annoy* or *irritate* should be used in the latter case.

allusion, illusion An *allusion* is a glancing reference to something, whereas an *illusion* is a fanciful idea that has no basis in fact. So one might speak of Shakespeare's *allusions* to classical mythology but of an aging character's *illusion* that she is still young. Compare *allusion* with *reference*.

alot There is no such word. *A lot* is standard. But the phrase is informal in any case and probably should not be used in a formal context (for instance, in term papers).

already, all ready Already means *by a specific time; all ready* means *entirely ready for*. Therefore,

The restaurant was *already* packed by six o'clock.

The staff was *all ready* by five.

alright This is not (yet) an acceptable spelling. *All right* is still common usage.

altogether, all together *Altogether* means *entirely, wholly; all together* means *in a group:*

I think that classes are *altogether* a waste of time.

The members of the chorus sang *all together* for once.

among, between *Between* is used with comparisons involving elements taken two at a time, even if they are part of a larger group. *Among* is used with comparisons involving three or more elements.

We had to choose *between* Oscar and Celia.

We had to choose *among* four applicants.

A decision was finally reached *between* the four partners. [that is, in private consultation, two by two]

An agreement was reached *among* the four partners at their annual meeting.

amount, number *Amount of* is used before a singular noun; *number of* is used before a plural noun:

Having a large *amount of money* is every American's dream.

Having a large *number of* thousand dollar bills is my dream.

and/or   Should be used sparingly and only when multiple choices are in fact possible. For instance, "We could go to the zoo *and/or* the museum" is acceptable, for there are indeed three possibilities allowed by the statement: the zoo or the museum or the zoo and the museum. However, "We couldn't decide *and/or* act on the measure" is not acceptable. Because a decision must come before an action based on it, there are no alternatives possible here. The statement should be revised: "We couldn't decide on the measure and so we couldn't act on it."

as, like   When it is used by itself (as opposed to being used in such combinations as *such as, as for, as to,* and *so as*), *as* functions primarily as a subordinating conjunction:

As everyone knows, Mary is *as tall as Bill (is).*

As I was saying, people usually behave *as they like.*

Like, on the other hand, is basically a verb or a preposition. We're interested in its use as a preposition:

You acted *like a fool* last night.

Like a comet, I'll rush back to you.

Like, then, is a preposition (or a verb) but not (in ordinary written discourse) a conjunction. In writing, avoid using *like* for *as, as if, as though:*

She ate *like* she had never eaten before. (nonstandard)

She ate *as if* (*as though*) she had never eaten before. (standard)

As, however, can also be a preposition meaning "functions as or in the role or capacity of":

As functions primarily *as* a subordinating conjunction.

The children dressed up *as* ghosts on Halloween.

He works *as* a dog.

The last sentence is silly, but it does make sense: the person in question makes a living by putting on a dog suit and playing the part of a dog all day. But it does not mean "He works *like* a dog."

Because of the difference in meaning, no one would probably confuse the prepositions *like* and *as.* But people do confuse the preposition *like* and the subordinating conjunction *as.* Here is a simple test for you to tell which to use in most cases: if a verb follows soon after, use *as;* if a verb does not follow soon after, use *like.*

Why don't you behave *as* a young person *should?*

The old man behaves *like* a young person.

The melody was sweet, *as* a melody *should be.*

The melody was sweet, *like* no melody (that) I had ever heard before.

The last example might seem like an exception, but it isn't. For the verb *had heard* does not come soon after *like.* In fact, the verb falls in a separate clause entirely, one modifying *melody*, whereas *like no melody* modifies *sweet.* So, again, if a verb comes soon after *as/like*, use *as;* if a verb does not come soon after, use *like.* You will almost always be right by so doing.

awhile, a while *Awhile* is an adverb whereas *a while* is an article (a) and a noun:

Can't you stay *awhile?*

I can stay for *a while.*

beside, besides *Beside* means "by the side of" whereas *besides* means "in addition to":

Who sat *beside* you at the meeting?

Who came to the meeting *besides* you?

between See *among.*

bring, take One *brings to* but *takes away:*

Bring your notebook to class and *take* it home after school.

cannot, can not *Cannot* means that one is unable to do something; *can not*, in contrast, means that one reserves the right not to do something:

I know what you want me to do, but I *can not* do it if I choose.

I know what you want me to do, but I'm afraid I *cannot* do it right now.

The first use is rare. Therefore, just use *cannot* and don't worry about the distinction.

center around Just as one *focuses on* and not *around*, one should *center on* and not *around.* Think of it this way: if you were shooting arrows at a target, you would want to center on the target and not around it.

comparative and superlative forms of adjectives and adverbs Adjectives and adverbs both have comparative and superlative states. Adjectives of one syllable and most of two syllables form their comparative and superlative states with the addition of *-er* and *-est*, respectively: *rich, richer, richest; pretty, prettier, prettiest.* Some two-syllable adjectives (for instance, those that end in *-er*), all adjectives of three or more syllables, and most adverbs (those ending in *-ly*) form their comparative and superlative states with *more* and *most*, respectively: *meager, more meager, most meager; expendable, more expendable, most expendable; gently, more gently, most gently.* Adverbs not ending in *-ly* take *-er* and *-est:* "That ship moves *fast/faster* than the other ships/*fastest* of all the ships in the harbor." The comparative and superlative forms of a few adjectives and adverbs are irregular: *bad, worse, worst; good/well, better, best; many/much, more, most; little, less, least.*

The comparative degree is used in comparisons of two things, the superlative with more than two: "We had *little* to eat/ *less* than our neighbors/the *least* of anybody. Double comparatives and superlatives, even though once acceptable, are not now and should be caught and corrected in proofreading: "Bud is the *more happier* of the two" should be changed to "Bud is the *happier* of the two"; "Sandra is the *most prettiest* girl I know" should be "Sandra is the *prettiest* girl I know."

Finally, some words do *not* have comparative and superlative forms. Here are a few: *absolute(ly), basic(ally), complete(ly), fundamental(ly), perfect(ly), ultimate(ly), unique(ly).* These and words like them express absolute states not open to comparison. Logically speaking, something is or isn't perfect, for instance, or is or isn't complete. That is, there are no degrees of being perfect or complete. There is, however, a way to express relative states with these words: use the word *nearly: more nearly complete, most nearly perfect.* With the word *nearly*, these absolute states remain absolute, for what is now being said is that one thing approaches the absolute state of completion more than another or that one thing approaches the absolute state of perfection more than do other things of the same kind. So logic is pacified and all is well.

compare to, compare with Use *compare(d) to* when speaking of a simple likeness observed by you or someone else; use *compare(d) with* when examining a likeness or a difference:

Milton *compares* the fallen angels *to* dead leaves in the fall.

We should *compare* this passage line by line *with* the manuscript version of the poem.

comparisons Have you ever wondered what advertisements mean when they say, for instance, "Our laundry detergent is 20 percent better" or

"Our scouring pad lasts 30 percent longer." *Better* and *longer* than what? I always complete such incomplete comparisons negatively: "Our laundry detergent is 20 percent better than the old crummy formula"; "Our scouring pad lasts 30 percent longer than it used to, when we were skimping on materials." At any rate, incomplete comparisons are either dishonest, as they are in advertisements, or sloppy and thoughtless, as they are in student writing. By "thoughtless" I mean "without thought" and also "discourteous with regard to the reader," for incomplete comparisons are generally confusing. So be conscious of what you are doing and, when using words that entail comparison like *more, better, fewer, less,* be sure to complete the comparison that such words instigate. Don't write, "I like this poem because it is easier"; write, "I like this poem because it is easier than that poem." The criterion of judgment may be faulty, but at least the construction is sound.

continual, continuous   *Continual* should be used with regard to something that recurs, *continuous* with regard to something that does not stop. Thus, "My clock chimes continually, both on the hour and the half hour" but "I hear a continuous ringing in my ears that never lets up."

criteria   See *data.*

data   Some English words derived from Latin and Greek become plural by substituting *-a* for the singular ending *-on* or *-um: criterion, datum, medium,* and *phenomenon* are four such words, their plurals being *criteria, data, media,* and *phenomena.* These plural forms should not be mistakenly used as singular nouns: "The *media plans* an exciting season this year"; "The *data* on the subject *is* convincing." If you mean "the mass media," use *media* and a plural verb; but if you mean "TV," as many seem to when they say *media,* then just say "TV." *Data,* on the other hand, is almost always what is meant, so you don't have to think much about the singular *datum.* Just remember that the word *data* is plural and calls for a plural verb. Ditto *criteria, phenomena,* and most other such words ending in *-a.*

different than   Just as one thing *differs from* another, one thing should be said to be *different from* another. Anyway, American usage calls for *different from* rather than *different than.*

differ from, differ with   If you *differ from* someone, you are unalike; if you *differ with* someone, you disagree. *Differ from,* then, means *different; differ with* means *to disagree.*

disinterested Do not confuse this fine word with *uninterested,* which means simply *not interested in, indifferent. Disinterested,* in contrast, means *impartial,* or *interested in a dispassionate way.* It is a fine thing to be disinterested. It is something to strive for.

don't *Do* is an irregular verb conjugated in the present thus: I do/you do/he, she, it (Edward, Nancy, the couch) does/we do/you do/they do. Therefore, one can say *I don't* or *we don't* but not (at least not and remain within the bounds of grammar and usage) *he don't* or *the couch don't.* For singular nouns and pronouns in the third person, use *doesn't: she doesn't; the couch doesn't.* Whether rightly so or not, by the way, many people would think you uneducated for using *don't* incorrectly.

double negatives Though, like double comparatives and superlatives, double negatives were once acceptable (Shakespeare abounds with all three), double negatives are no longer sanctioned by usage. Therefore, they should be expunged from anything you write. "Pay me no never mind," for instance, should be changed to "Pay me no mind"; "You don't have no ice" should be "You don't have any ice"; "Gretchen didn't give me none" should be "Gretchen didn't give me any"; and "I don't have nothing to do" should be changed to "I don't have anything to do." In that words like *hardly* and *scarcely* themselves express negative states, a sentence like "I can't hardly/scarcely walk up the stairs" should be "I can hardly/scarcely walk up the stairs."

effect See *affect.*

else See *other.*

etc. There are several points that need to be made about this word. (1) Since *etc.* means "and other things," *and etc.* is redundant. (2) Do not use *etc.* after saying *like* or *such as:* "Sports *like/such as* soccer and football, *etc.,* require much energy." *Like* and *such as* suggest by themselves that there are other sports that fall in the same category; therefore, *etc.* is redundant. (3) *Etc.* should not be used as a catchall, standing in for something the writer should have said: "So we see that banks, savings plans, *etc.,* should be monitored by the government." *Etc.* can be used in an instance like this only if all of the institutions in question have already been specified. (4) Many teachers and writers now prefer *and so forth* and *and so on* to *etc.* But note that even if you use one or the other, points (2) and (3) still apply.

everyday, every day *Everyday* is an adjective whereas *every day* is an adverb:

> The milkman used to come *every day*.
>
> Don't dress up. This is just an *everyday* affair.

except See *accept.*

explicit, implicit *Explicit* means that a meaning is right there, open, on the surface, direct. *Implicit* means much the reverse—that the meaning of something is indirect, implied, not immediately on the surface. So you might conclude that an advertisement *explicitly* tells why a certain car is the one to buy but that the *implicit* message of the advertisement, which features a sports car and a bevy of beautiful girls, is that if the male viewer buys the car in question, then the girls will follow. Most works of literature, along with advertisements and other types of propaganda, have both explicit and implicit meanings.

famous See *infamous.*

firstly, secondly, thirdly Because *first, second, third* and so forth are themselves adverbs, *firstly, secondly, thirdly,* and so forth are redundant. Use *first, second, third,* and so forth instead. For the last item, you may say *last* or *finally.*

good, well *Good* is always an adjective: "That's a *good hat* you have there." Therefore, *good* should never be used as an adverb: "We work good together." In contrast, *well* may be an adjective or an adverb: "We *work well* together" (adverb); "*Everything* is *well*" (adjective). In one construction, both are possible but different in meaning:

> I feel well.
>
> I feel good.

The first is a statement about one's state of health; the second is a statement about one's psychological state, or state of feelings.

hanged, hung A picture is *hung* but a person is *hanged.* The past and past participles of each verb differ (*hang, hung, hung* versus *hang, hanged, hanged*); each must be used accordingly.

hopefully Meaning *full of hope,* this word should clearly not be used to mean *it is to be hoped,* as it so often is: "Hopefully, we shall arrive before the conference begins." This means "We shall be full of hope when we arrive, which will be before the conference begins." If that isn't what is meant, the statement should be revised: "We hope to arrive before the conference begins." Straightforward and simple—that's always the best way.

illusion See *allusion*.

implicit See *explicit*.

imply, infer An author *implies*; a reader *infers*. Therefore, do not say that you *imply* something from a text. You *infer* what it *implies*.

in, into *In* means *within*; *into* means *to the inside of*:

> I found what I needed *in* the book you gave me.
> We went *into* the woods for a picnic.

infamous A person can be *famous, infamous,* or *notorious. Famous* has positive associations; *infamous* and *notorious* are both negative. In other words, it is good to be famous but not so good to be *infamous* or *notorious*.

infer See *imply*.

inflammable *Flammable* is the right word.

irregardless *Irregardless* is a double negative. Use *regardless*.

is when, is where Both are ungrammatical, for *is* links a noun with another noun or with an adjective, but *where* and *when* are adverbial. Therefore, do not write, for instance:

> A dictionary *is where* words are defined.
> Photosynthesis *is when* plants convert light to food.

Instead, write something like:

> A dictionary is a book in which words are defined.
> Words are defined in a dictionary.
> Photosynthesis occurs when plants convert light to food.
> Photosynthesis is the process whereby plants convert light to food.

its, it's *Its* is a possessive pronoun; *it's* is a contraction for *it is*:

> The dog had *its* muzzle on when I passed.
> *It's* a lovely day today.

kind(s), types When singular, use *this* or *that* (*this kind of, that type of*); when plural, use *these* or *those* (*these kinds of, those types of*). Further, you must carefully think through what you wish to say when you use one of these phrases, for there are several possible ways of using them and each has a different meaning: *this type of construction*, *these types of constructions*, and *these types of construction*, for instance, are not interchangeable. The first points to a specific construction and the second to specific constructions, whereas the third points to *construction* as an idea, or that which gives rise to all specific constructions. Finally, don't write *kind of a* or *type of a*. The *a* is unidiomatic and superfluous in any case.

like *Like* is a word that is often used ungrammatically and, indeed, meaninglessly: "Like I say, . . . ," " . . . like it is," "It's like, well, y'know," "I was—like—scared because my parents would—like—be furious." This is non-language, *like* in each case being nothing more than a stutter. Avoid the word used in ways like these. See *as, like*.

literally The word means *to the letter* and covers everything the opposite of *figuratively*. Therefore, to say, for instance, that "Hodgkins literally blew his top" is absurd, for the statement is figurative and not literal at all. In other words, *literally* should not be used as an intensifier but only as a word that underscores the literal aspect of a statement: "My father *literally* washed out my mouth with soap."

maybe, may be *Maybe* is an adverb; *may be* is a verb:

　　Maybe I'll see you on the bus.

　　The class *may be* canceled because of the funeral.

media See *data*.

nauseated, nauseous Do not use *nauseous* when you mean *nauseated*. *Nauseated* means *to be sick*; *nauseous* means *to make sick*:

　　I became *nauseated* because of the *nauseous* odor.

Remember, should you say "I am *nauseous*," you'll be saying that you cause other people to become ill.

no, nor Use *nor* with *neither: neither house nor home*; use *or* with *no: no food or drink*.

notorious See *infamous*.

number See *amount*.

of *Might of, could of, should of, would of*, and so forth, are substandard. Do not use *of* instead of *have*.

other, else Remember to use *other/else* in comparisons of one member of a class of things or people with other members of the same class:

Mildred is stronger than any *other* member of her wrestling team.

Stanley is brighter than anyone *else* in his class.

Without *other* and *else*, these statements are illogical in that one cannot be stronger or brighter than oneself.

past, passed *Past* may be used as a noun ("I often think of the *past*"), an adjective ("The *past* tense is my favorite"), or a preposition ("Drive *past* the gas station and you'll find my house"). *Past* may not be used as a verb. *Passed* is the past tense of *pass*.

phenomena See *data*.

principal, principle "The princi*pal* is your *pal*," school teachers used to say. That's a good way of remembering the difference. *Principal* means *main* (as in the *principal* parts of a verb) or *head official* (like the *principal* of a school). *Principle* means *a basic truth or standard:* "I do not compromise my *principles*."

reason is because Because the linking verb *to be* requires a noun or an adjective after it, *is because* will not do. The reason it won't is that *because* is adverbial. Anyway, *the reason is because* is redundant, for it means *the reason is the reason*. Use, instead, *the reason is that*. That solves the problem on both counts.

The reason I couldn't go *is that* I had cholera.

reference, allusion A *reference* is an *overt* mention of a name, place, period of time, or whatever. "The Babe Ruth of song writers," for instance, contains a *reference* to Babe Ruth. An *allusion*, in contrast, is *not* overt. It is an implied or indirect reference to something in the culture at large that the writer assumes the reader will know. "This is a whale of a novel, a great white whale," for instance, *alludes* to Melville's *Moby Dick*.

so, so that *So* should be used as a coordinating conjunction with a comma before it:

We built the house out of brick, *so* it should withstand high winds.

If you don't use the comma, don't use *so*; use *so that*:

We built the house out of brick *so that* it would withstand high winds.

As a conjunction, *so* is the equivalent of *therefore*; in *so that*, *so* means *with the purpose*. The meanings are not the same.

so, such Each should be followed by a *that* clause:

> It was *so* cold *that* we froze.
> It was *such* a cold day *that* we froze.

Do not use either as an intensifier:

> It was *so* cold.
> It was *such* a cold day.

The reader expects a *that* clause to follow each and will feel that something is missing if the clause isn't provided. Also, the two words are weak, so they don't work well as intensifiers in any case.

subsequently This should not be mistaken for *consequently*. *Subsequently* refers to a time period, *consequently* to a result.

superlative See *comparative and superlative*.

suppose to, use to Both are substandard. Write *supposed to* and *used to*.

take See *bring*.

that, which *That* should be used to head restrictive relative clauses and *which* to head nonrestrictive relative clauses:

> There's the house *that* I was telling you about.
> We caught the midnight train, *which* stops in Chicago.

In any case, use *which* sparingly (for it's terribly formal) and leave *that* out whenever it can be readily inferred from the context. For instance,

> That's the kind of car (that) I want.

their, they're, there *Their* is the possessive form of *they*; *they're* is a contraction of *they are*; and *there* is an adverb of place. Each should be used thus:

> *Their* cat scratched me.
> *They're* coming for dinner on Sunday.
> *There* is the coat I've been looking for.

then, than *Then* is an adverb of time; *than* is a conjunction that introduces a comparison:

> Jones said that she couldn't do the job *then* because of other commitments.
> One job was much greater *than* the other.

Using *then* for *than* or vice versa may seem like a minor error to you, but it could cost you most if not all of your readers. It's the kind of mistake that makes the reader distrust the writer and become leery of what he or she has to say.

thusly The word is grammatically redundant and fussy. Never use it. Use *thus*, the proper adverb, instead.

to, too, two A confusion of one of these words with another can be terribly puzzling for the reader. For instance, an aunt of mine writes, "I'm quitting my job as president of my church group. They don't want me too. They say I've done such a wonderful job." Then why don't they want her? One has to puzzle out that she meant "They don't want me to quit." If you have a problem with these words, then be sure to proofread everything you write with them in mind.

type See *kind*.

use to See *suppose to*.

vary, very *Vary* is a verb meaning *to give variety to; very* is an adjective or adverb generally used as an intensifier:

> I *vary* what I have for breakfast.
>
> That's the *very* best hat I have.

If you follow my advice, you won't have trouble with this pair: don't use *very* at all. The word has been used so often that it no longer really intensifies. In fact, it might just do the reverse. It has become pallid, and how can something that itself is pallid intensify? Just write, "That's my best hat" and leave it at that. Your writing will have more impact if you get rid of weak epithets like *very*.

well See *good*.

which See *that, which*.

whose, who's *Whose* is a possessive pronoun; *who's* is the contraction of *who is:*

> This is the man *whose* daughter you met.
>
> *Who's* the young lady you met?

your, your're *Your* is the possessive form of *you; you're* is the contraction of *you are:*

> *Your* mother called and left a message for *your* father.
>
> I hope *you're* not intending to go out like that!

A Brief Guide to the Use and Documentation of Sources and Related Matters

USING SOURCES

Plagiarism

Plagiarism is the unacknowledged use—whether intentional or not—of another person's words or ideas. What you should know first about the use of source material is that anything not your own in a paper will be considered plagiarized if it is not attributed properly. Every direct quotation must be either put within quotation marks or blocked and indented, and a citation must be given referring to a Works Cited list at the end of your paper. Summaries and paraphrases also call for citations. If you cite your sources appropriately, there will be no problem. If you don't, your theft—for that is what it will be—will most likely be caught. Plagiarism usually shouts its presence, especially if the student has lifted something from a published text. Even if the instructor does not know the source, plagiarism can be recognized on stylistic or ideational grounds alone. And how silly plagiarism is. It insults the intelligence of the reader and shows that the student has completely misunderstood the purpose of research. When you do research, proudly show the work you've done by your citations. What is impressive is how you use your sources to buttress *your* ideas.

Referring to Titles

The way titles are quoted is simple: as a general rule, the title of something published in a longer work with a title of its own is put within quotation marks; the title of anything published as an independent unit is italicized (underlined in a typed text). For instance, the title of any short essay in this book should be put in quotation marks: "The Jaspers," "My Summer Job." Should you refer to the book as a whole, underline its title: The Organized Writer. The titles of books, newspapers, and magazines are underlined; the titles of chapters within books, articles in magazines, short stories and lyric poems, and so forth are put in quotation marks. Incidentally, just as quotation marks and italics (underlining) are not used in titles of the works themselves, you should use neither when you place your own title at the head of your paper. However, if your paper title *includes* a story or book title, these should be put in quotation marks or underlined, as appropriate. Here are two examples of paper titles containing titles of published works:

Symbolism in Frost's "The Road Not Taken"

The Pitfalls of Metaphor as defined in The Organized Writer

Remember that *your whole* title should not have quotation marks around it or be underlined (unless, of course, your title consists of nothing but the title of the work you are writing about—a practice almost always to be discouraged).

Continuous versus Blocked Quotations

When quoting from a source, you must make a decision depending upon what is being quoted and how much of it. That is, one or two lines of verse and up to four lines of prose should be put in quotation marks and typed so as to be continuous with your text. The following exemplifies this mode of quotation and the way it looks: I began this paragraph by saying, "When quoting from a source, you must make a decision depending upon what is being quoted and how much of it." However, more than four lines of prose (or more than two lines of verse) should be blocked and indented—that is, separated from the lines of your own writing and indented from the left ten spaces. Such quotations are often introduced by a clause ending in a colon, though other punctuation, or even none, may sometimes serve, depending on how the beginning of the quoted text flows grammatically from your own text. The following blocked quotation illustrates these points.

Proffitt first asks why the speaker of Frost's "The Road Not Taken" "go[es] on to say, 'I took the one less traveled by,'" and then answers as follows:

> Of course, he says no such thing. Look at the last stanza . . . and observe its tense. What the speaker actually says is that sometime in the future he *will* say, "I took the one less traveled by." In other words, in years to come he will forget the truth of the matter and will rationalize his choice thus.

Such is the look of blocked quotations. Each quotation, note, would need to be followed by a parenthetical citation, but we'll consider that matter later in this appendix. Note, too, that there are no quotation marks around the material blocked; the blocking itself signals quotation. Another note of caution: do not use long quotations to excess. Summarize and paraphrase whenever possible. Use your sources for evidence, not padding.

A quotation within a blocked quotation—that is, something quoted by the author of your source—is put within normal (double) quotation marks (" "). In continuous quotations, interior quotations go within single quotation marks (' ') as follows:

> Proffitt says, "What the speaker actually says is that . . . he *will* say, 'I took the one less traveled by.'"

Observe the punctuation here. In American English, periods and commas always go *inside* the closing quotation mark(s) thus: "I took the one less traveled by," says Frost; Proffitt says, "What the speaker actually says is that . . . he *will* say, 'I took the one less traveled by.'" In contrast, semicolons and colons go outside: He said, "No, I can't"; he also said, "I wouldn't if I could." Exclamation points and question marks go inside if they are part of the quotation and outside if they are your own.

Changing Punctuation

There are, then, two minor changes of punctuation that you can and often must make with respect to continuous quotations: (1) if quotation marks are found *within* the material you are quoting, change those quotation marks from double (" ") to single (' ') ones; (2) if necessary to make the quotation fit smoothly into your sentence, use a comma (or ellipsis dots—see the next subsection) within the closing quotation marks even though the original may have had no mark of punctuation there or some other mark, such as a period, that you will be replacing with the comma. Consider, for instance, the punctuation changes one would have to make in quoting the following lines from Robert Browning's poem "My Last Duchess":

> Frà Pandolf chanced to say, "Her mantle laps
> Over my lady's wrist too much," or. . . .

Now the lines as they would be quoted:

> The poem's speaker says, "Frà Pandolf chanced to say, 'Her mantle laps/Over my lady's wrist too much.'"

Note that the original double quotation marks have been changed to single marks; and the comma after "much" in the poem has been changed to a period to make Browning's lines fit into their new context.

Ellipsis and Square Brackets

Quotations must be exact, except for the two minor changes of punctuation we've just mentioned in connection with continuing quotations. However, quotations need not be complete. You can quote anything you like, from a paragraph or more down to a phrase or even a word. You can also leave words out of a quotation or add words of your own. The first is accomplished by ellipsis. For instance, let's say you wish to quote the first sentence of this subsection so as to impart the gist of its meaning. Your sentence might look like this: "Quotations must be exact, except for . . . minor changes of punctuation." Usually not used at the beginning of a quotation (for the reader knows that every quotation is an excerpt) and not necessarily used at the end, ellipsis entails the use of three spaced dots to show that something from a source has been left out (only three dots, note, except when an ellipsis is indicated at the end of a sentence, in which case the period is also required).

If you wish to insert words of your own into a quotation for some reason—to make the quotation fit smoothly into your context, perhaps, or to comment on something within the quotation—you can do so by the use of square brackets. Let me exemplify each situation.

> Proffitt first asks why Frost's speaker "go[es] on to say, 'I took the one less traveled by.'"

Proffitt says that "If you wish to insert words of your own into a quotation [note this] . . . you can do so by the use of square brackets."

Fitting Quotations with Contexts

A quotation must be exact, yet—as we've noted—it must also fit smoothly into the context in which you are putting it. Often the context, the quotation, or both must be adjusted to make the necessary accommodation. A quotation can be adjusted by ellipsis, by additions in brackets, and by paraphrase (that is, what does not grammatically fit your context can be restated in your own words and the rest quoted). Your own context can also be adjusted. For instance, if you were quoting the sentence "I find no reason to alter my opinion," you would not want to write:

The author states that he "find no reason to alter my opinion."

The quotation is exact but, in its new context, ungrammatical and confusing. The problem might be solved in various ways. One way would be to change your own sentence by adding the word *could* (which fits grammatically with the quotation's first word, *find*) and by making a bracketed insertion in the quotation itself to change *my* to *his* (the brackets alert the reader that the word is yours, not in the original source):

The author states that he could "find no reason to alter [his] opinion."

Introducing Quotations

In your remarks introducing a quotation, you will usually want to incorporate the name of the person being quoted, and in any case you will want to make sure that the reason for your quotation is immediately clear. If the reason may not be clear, introduce the quotation by briefly suggesting why you are using it in the present context. For instance, let's say that in a paper on Frost's "The Road Not Taken" you write:

In "The Road Not Taken," the imagery of the road and the fork in the road is both concrete and symbolic. "No ideas but in things."

You would need to revise this statement to introduce the quotation, for here it just sits, a puzzlement to the reader and so an obstacle to you achieving your purpose. Note how, in the following revision, introducing the quotation makes its purpose and thus its meaning clear:

> In "The Road Not Taken," the imagery of the road and the fork in the road is both concrete and symbolic. Something William Carlos Williams said sheds light on Frost's use of concrete imagery: "No ideas but in things."

You would need, of course, to add a parenthetical citation to the source of the line being quoted—a procedure we shall consider shortly.

Quotation, Summary, and Paraphrase

Quotation is not the only way, or always the best way, to present the ideas of another. Often a summary or a paraphrase will prove more effective. A summary is a condensation of someone else's thinking down to the core of that person's idea. For instance, the paragraph headed "Fitting Quotations with Contexts" on page 172 could be summarized as follows: Proffitt emphasizes that quotations must fit smoothly into their new contexts. A paraphrase is more elaborate but is still a condensation in that it restates someone else's thought in brief. A paraphrase of the paragraph on context that we just summarized would be something like this: As Proffitt emphasizes, in order to make a quotation fit smoothly into its new context—and it is important for the writer to do so—the context itself can be adjusted by, for instance, the use of paraphrase, and the quotation can be adjusted by ellipsis or by addition in square brackets.

Observe that the paraphrase, like the summary, is restricted to the ideas in the source and that the paraphrase follows its sequence of ideas. Be sure to be alert and recognize that you are summarizing or paraphrasing if you are. Then provide the proper citation.

SOURCES: PRIMARY AND SECONDARY

Sources can be divided into *primary* and *secondary*. A primary source is just that: it is a work that comes *first*. In a paper on "The Road Not Taken," for instance, "The Road Not Taken" would be a primary source. So would any document by Frost—a letter, say, or a journal in which he wrote about the poem. Secondary sources include works of commentary, criticism, history, and so forth. What you need to remember is that primary sources are direct evidence and secondary sources are not. One uses secondary sources to bolster an argument and to lend authority to one's views. But just because so and so said such and such in a published book or periodical does not make it so. Finally, the only valid evidence is the primary source, and secondary sources should not be used to substitute for grappling with a primary text, which alone can give rise to a worthwhile paper.

CITING SOURCES

Whether you are quoting directly, summarizing, or paraphrasing, you must provide an appropriate citation in your text. The dual purpose of any citation is to acknowledge your borrowing as smoothly and concisely as possible within the text and to enable your reader to locate full information about your source in a list called Works Cited, which is arranged alphabetically by authors' last names at the end of your paper. Thus the key element of a citation within your paper is the author's last name, together with the specific page number(s) on which the cited material appears in the source.

Put the author's last name the page reference (the page or pages on which the material you are quoting, summarizing, or paraphrasing can be found) in parentheses at the end of the quotation, summary, or paraphrase:

> "Whether you are quoting directly, summarizing, or paraphrasing, you must provide an appropriate citation in your text" (Proffitt 174).

> Quotations must fit smoothly into their new context (Proffitt 172).

Often it is smoother, however, to mention the author's name in introducing the summary, paraphrase, or quotation, in which case you need not repeat the name in the parenthetical citation; the page reference alone is then enough:

> As Proffitt says, "Whether you are quoting directly, summarizing, or paraphrasing, you must provide an appropriate citation in your text" (174).

> Proffitt stresses that quotations must fit smoothly in their new context (172).

Parenthetical citation is used for books, stories, articles, poems, and newspapers alike, with more detailed information left for the Works Cited list put at the end of a paper (we shall take up this matter shortly).

Citing Continuous versus Blocked Quotations

There is one small difference between citations coming after continuous quotations and those coming after blocked quotations. When citations for continuous quotations come at the ends of sentences (as they most often do), the sentence period comes *after* the citation, as in the following example: "My Summer Job" is ironic from first to last (McMahon 86). With blocked quotations, on the other hand, the period comes at the end of the quotation, and the citation stands alone two spaces to the right of the period. Here, for instance, are the first sentences of the previous subsection as they would appear and be cited in a blocked quotation:

> Whether you are quoting directly, summarizing, or paraphrasing, you must provide an appropriate citation in your text. The dual purpose of any citation is to acknowledge your borrowing as smoothly and concisely as possible within the text and to enable your reader to locate full information about your source in a list called Works Cited, which is arranged alphabetically by authors' last names at the end of your paper. (Proffitt 174)

Three Problem Spots

There are a few other matters concerning citation that you will need to know when doing a properly documented paper. If you have parenthetical citations for two or more works by the same author, then each citation must include not only the author's last name but also a short form of the title of the work (followed, of course, by the page reference). For instance, in a paper that contained the following references to two different essays found in this book by Sandra Calvi, "My Dog" and "So Much for Philosophy!" here is how the citations would be handled:

> Sandra Calvi says that she "often think[s] that a dog is a better companion than a man" ("Dog" 19).

> "Benito didn't look for an answer," we're told, but "just sat there smiling" (Calvi, "Philosophy" 102).

Without the short designation in the citation, the reader would not be able to tell which of the two essays by Calvi is being referred to in each case. Of course, if the author or the work or both are identified in the sentence itself, neither the one nor the other nor both need appear in the citation.

A somewhat similar problem is that of two or more authors having the same last name. In this case, each citation must include the first name or initial of the author, as follows: (P. J. Levins), (Hal Levins).

Further, in citing an anonymous work such as a news report, use instead of the author's name the first word or phrase (omitting initial articles *A*, *An*, or *The*) of the title of the piece, followed by the page reference: ("Myth" 112) for a citation to page 112 to an article entitled "Myth and the Mythic Mind" in *The Book of All Mythologies*. The reader will be able to locate the full reference in the Works Cited list because anonymous works are alphabetized by the first word of their titles. Finally, a special case of the anonymous work is an article in an encyclopedia or other reference volume in which the articles are arranged alphabetically. When you cite these articles, no page reference is required because the reader can quickly look up the article in its alphabetical location. In sum, use common sense. The main purpose of parenthetical citation is to allow the reader to use the appended Works Cited list with ease. Everything done should serve this purpose.

THE WORKS CITED LIST

At the end of your paper, on its own page(s), should be a list called Works Cited containing an entry for each of the sources you have used. As we have seen, the information in the citations within your paper is abbreviated. In Works Cited you list your sources alphabetically by the last name of each author (or the title if there is no author indicated) and give your reader complete information for each source so that the reader can go to the source to confirm its validity or to study the subject further. There are a great many possible kinds of entries and so, naturally, a great many possible complications in getting a Works Cited list into shape. However, for our purposes—and, in fact, for the purposes of most people most of the time—only a few types of entry need be considered. We will examine here the most common types, especially those that will be valuable to you in using this book. A Works Cited list including the main examples discussed in this appendix appears at the conclusion (page 181). The style followed here, as throughout this appendix, is the one most commonly used in literature and composition courses, that of the Modern Language Association of America. (Some other styles are used in other disciplines.) Should you happen to need information beyond what is presented here, consult Joseph Gibaldi and Walter S. Achtert, *MLA Handbook for Writers of Research Papers*, 3rd ed., New York: MLA, 1988, which is sure to be in your college library.

Books and Journal Articles

The works most frequently cited are books and articles. An entry for a book should include the name of the author, last name first (if a work has two or more authors, names of authors after the first are straightforward); the full title of the work, including subtitle (separated from the title by a colon), underlined; the edition, if other than the first edition; and finally the city of publication followed by a colon, a shortened form of the publisher's name, and the date of publication. Here are two examples:

> Brooks, Cleanth, R. W. B. Lewis, and Robert Penn Warren. <u>American Literature: The Makers and the Making</u>. Shorter ed. New York: St. Martin's, 1974.
> Nowottny, Winifred. <u>The Language Poets Use</u>. London: Athlone, 1952.

When a work has more than three authors, give only the first author's name, followed by a comma and the phrase "et al." (not in quotation marks), which is Latin for "and others." For instance, had the first book listed had four authors rather than three, the author would have been given as follows: Brooks, Cleanth, et al.

For articles, treat the author's name exactly as for a book. Then comes the title of the article in quotation marks; next, the name of the journal, underlined; and finally the volume number, issue number, date of publication, and the inclusive page numbers of the article (not the page reference for your specific citation, which appears in parentheses in the text of your paper). For a daily, weekly, or monthly periodical, however, omit volume and issue numbers and give the specific date instead. Following are two typical entries:

> Funey, Sean. "Essays by Poets." <u>Journal of Lyric Poetry</u> 18.2 (1984): 23–41.
> Staggs, Sam. "James Dickey." <u>Publishers Weekly</u> 29 May 1987: 62–63.

In the entry for the Funey article, the volume number of the journal is 18, and the issue number is 2 (with this information, only the year of publication, 1984, is given); the article runs from page 23 to page 41. Because the Staggs entry is for a weekly publication, the specific date replaces the volume and issue number.

Observe the spacing in all four of the preceding entries: two spaces are used after each discrete item of information that is followed by a period—after the author's name, for example, and again after the title of the book or article, and still again after the edition, as in the entry for Brooks, Lewis, and Warren. The same would be true of other discrete items of information, such as the name of an editor or translator (as other examples in this appendix will show). Note, too, that the first line of an entry is not indented and the rest of the lines are indented five spaces.

Anthologies

For an anthology, give the editor's name, last name first (as for an author), followed by a comma, a space, and the abbreviation "ed." Then give the title and the rest of the information as for any other book. Such an entry looks like this:

```
Proffitt, Edward, ed.  The Organized Writer: A Brief
    Rhetoric.  Mountain View: Mayfield, 1991.
```

In a paper in which, for instance, you compare two stories found in the present text, this would be your main entry. How the individual stories would be entered in the list is covered in the next subsection.

A Work in an Anthology

For an essay or other selection found in a book like this (that is, a book that contains work by many hands) or found in a straight anthology, begin, if you have provided a main entry as just shown, with the author of the selection (in the usual way). Next give the selection title, followed by a period, in quotation marks (exception: titles of plays are underlined); if the selection is a translation, next give the translator's name preceded by "Trans."; and finally give the last name of the anthology's editor and the inclusive page numbers of the story or other selection as it appears in the anthology. Here are two examples:

```
Masucci, Tracy.  "Three Months with the Aboto."
    Proffitt 44-45.
```

> Ji-Hoon, Ahn. "The Air, the Water, the Waste." Trans.
>   Guy Faulks. Proffitt 87–88.

This kind of entry, referring to a main entry for the anthology itself (in this case the main entry for Proffitt shown in the preceding subsection), is convenient if you cite more than one selection from the same anthology; it saves you the trouble of repeating all the information about the anthology in the entry for each selection. However, if you refer to only one selection from the anthology, you will find it more efficient simply to use one full entry as follows:

> McKeever, Ciaran. "Self-Expression." The Organized
>   Writer: A Brief Rhetoric. Ed. Edward Proffitt.
>   Mountain View: Mayfield, 1991, 84–85.

Treat a *signed* article in an encyclopedia or other reference book as you would an article or story in a collection, except don't include the name of the editor of the reference work:

> Eble, Jane. "E. M. Forster and His Followers."
>   Encyclopaedia Britannica: Macropaedia. 1974 ed.

If the article is not signed or if you are listing a book with no author given, the name of the book or article should appear alphabetically thus:

> The Times Atlas of the World. 5th ed. New York: New
>   York Times, 1975.
> "Frost, Robert." The Columbia Encyclopaedia. 1950 ed.

Titles beginning with "A," "An," or "The" are alphabetized according to the second word of the title. Note, too, how an edition is indicated, and observe that if the materials within the source volume are arranged alphabetically you may omit volume and page numbers.

A Newspaper Article

To list an article from a newspaper, begin with the writer's name if specified (if not, begin with the title of the article), followed by the title of the article (the major headline) in quotation marks, the name of the paper (excluding initial *A, An,* or *The*) underlined, the complete date, the edition if an edition, and the section letter, if the paper is divided into sections, along with the inclusive page numbers if the article is continuous (see first example to follow) or the first page number followed by a plus sign if the article is continued after skipping pages (see second example).

> Crane, Stephen. "Captain Murphy's Shipwrecked Crew."
>   <u>Florida Times Union</u> 5 Jan. 1897: 1–2.
> "The Literate and the Damned." <u>Bar Harbour Post Dis-</u>
>   <u>patch</u> 12 July 1953, late ed.: B17+.

In the second entry, the article begins on page 17 of section B and then skips to a page farther back, as often happens in magazines and newspapers. Note, incidentally, that the names of all months except May, June, and July (in other words, all months with names more than four letters long) are abbreviated in Works Cited entries (*Jan.* in the first of the preceding entries, but *July* in the second).

Two or More Works by the Same Author

For two or more works by the same author, give the author's name or the first work and then, for the other works, use three typed hyphens in place of the author's name (the hyphens are followed by a period, as is the author's name). Arrange the words alphabetically by title.

> Masucci, Tracy. "A Matter of Face." Proffitt 85–86.
> ---. "Three Months with the Aboto." Proffitt 44–45.
> ---. <u>Details</u>. New York: Random, 1989.

When different books are involved, a full citation for each is necessary, though the author's name is still indicated by the three typed hyphens for the second and subsequent works in the list.

SAMPLE WORKS CITED LIST AND SAMPLE MANUSCRIPT

On the next page is a typewritten Works Cited list in the proper MLA format, listing all the works referred to in the preceding discussions. Study it carefully and be sure that you understand the entries individually and also the reasons for the order in which they are presented. Following this sample list is the sample essay on Frost's "The Road Not Taken" from pages 72–74 of this book, now revised (for the purpose of illustration) to incorporate documented sources and typewritten in MLA format so that you can see how margins, spacing, page numbering, and other matters are handled.

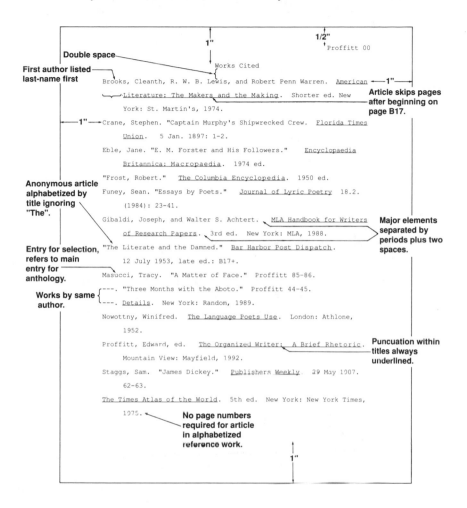

1/2"
Proffitt 00

1"

Double space

Works Cited

First author listed last-name first

Brooks, Cleanth, R. W. B. Lewis, and Robert Penn Warren. American ◄──1"──►
Literature: The Makers and the Making. Shorter ed. New
York: St. Martin's, 1974.

Article skips pages after beginning on page B17.

◄──1"──► Crane, Stephen. "Captain Murphy's Shipwrecked Crew. Florida Times
Union. 5 Jan. 1897: 1-2.

Eble, Jane. "E. M. Forster and His Followers." Encyclopaedia
Britannica: Macropaedia. 1974 ed.

Anonymous article alphabetized by title ignoring "The".

"Frost, Robert." The Columbia Encyclopedia. 1950 ed.

Funey, Sean. "Essays by Poets." Journal of Lyric Poetry 18.2.
(1984): 23-41.

Gibaldi, Joseph, and Walter S. Achtert. MLA Handbook for Writers
of Research Papers. 3rd ed. New York: MLA, 1988.

Major elements separated by periods plus two spaces.

Entry for selection, refers to main entry for anthology.

"The Literate and the Damned." Bar Harbor Post Dispatch.
12 July 1953, late ed.: B17+.

Masucci, Tracy. "A Matter of Face." Proffitt 85-86.

Works by same author.

---. "Three Months with the Aboto." Proffitt 44-45.
---. Details. New York: Random, 1989.

Nowottny, Winifred. The Language Poets Use. London: Athlone,
1952.

Proffitt, Edward, ed. The Organized Writer: A Brief Rhetoric.
Mountain View: Mayfield, 1992.

Puncuation within titles always underlined.

Staggs, Sam. "James Dickey." Publishers Weekly. 29 May 1007.
62-63.

The Times Atlas of the World. 5th ed. New York: New York Times,
1075.

No page numbers required for article in alphabetized reference work.

1"

Firstname Surname

Professor Wise

English 102, sec. 14

October 11, 1991

The Problem of Choice

Well over a hundred years ago, the British philosopher John
Stuart Mill defined "modern" in connection with the freedom of
choice: "human beings are no longer born to their place in life,"
Mill observed, "but are free to employ their faculties . . . to
achieve the lot that may appear to them most desirable" (143).
Our lives are no longer mapped out by tradition; we have the
luxury of being able to choose what college to attend, whom we
shall marry, what occupation to pursue. But upon what grounds can
we make such choices? There's the rub. Our precious freedom most
often leaves us in a quandary: we are reluctant to choose and then
ambivalent about the choices we've made. As Eric Fromm puts it,
"We disguise our real motives, but underneath it all, what drives
most of us is a desire to escape from the burden of our liberty"
(Escape 7). In "The Road Not Taken," Robert Frost dramatizes the
difficulty of this burden by way of a speaker who is representative of us human beings loosed from tradition but not comfortable
with this relatively new freedom of ours.

Before we turn to Frost's speaker, however, it should be
noted that the situation Frost describes is symbolic, as most
readers probably understand intuitively. Traveling down a road
generally symbolizes (in our culture, at least) life's journey,
and a fork in the road signifies an important choice to be made as
to the subsequent direction of one's life. This age-old symbolism

is so common in our culture as to need no further comment. It
should be remarked, though, that Frost uses these symbols with
great skill: his treatment of them makes them seem fresh and newly
meaningful. In the words of John Lynen, "In 'The Road Not Taken,'
Frost incorporates common symbolism in a most uncommon way"
(182-83).

But to return to the poem's speaker, he expresses one reason
for his difficulty in choosing his road at the beginning of the
poem when he says, "sorry I could not travel both" (line 2). That
is, he didn't wish to make a choice at all. (His regret at having
to choose, incidentally, is implied as well by the poem's title.)
Confronted with an important choice, most of us feel the same; we
would eat our cake and have it too. When asked what she might
like to be, a child I know replied: "a policewoman, a reporter, a
ballet dancer, and a doctor." Along the line, of course, she will
narrow her list down, finally, to one occupation, but probably
with a certain sense of narrowness and of lost possibilities.
Hans Loewald touches the heart of the matter:

> Growing means giving up as well as gaining. As we move
> into adulthood ..., we gain the power that comes with
> specialization but we lose the freedom of potentiality.
> We purchase solidity of self ... at the expense of a
> progressive narrowing of focus. (57)

Surely, this is true. And to some extent, surely, we all regret
not being able to take all of the roads before us. At any rate,
the speaker's difficulty in choosing--as that difficulty stems
from his wishing not to limit his possibilities--is internal, an

aspect of the psychology of the chooser rather than inherent in the things he must choose between.

But this second potential source of difficulty, a source external to the self, is suggested as well as the poem moves on. Though the speaker says that one of the two roads "was grassy and wanted wear" (8), he immediately refutes himself by saying that in fact the two roads were exactly the same, equally worn and equally covered "In leaves no step had trodden black" (12). So, really, there was no rational basis for a choice of a road. This kind of difficulty is inherent externally in the things that must be chosen between. But, as one critic observes, "In Frost generally, choice entails external difficulties interacting with internal proclivities" (Proffitt 249). Specifically, the speaker's reaction to the sameness of the roads (an external difficulty) takes us again to the internal sphere, and once again we see that the speaker's thought and feeling are marked by reluctance and ambivalence--expressed now by the speaker's desire to keep the other road "for another day" (13). With so little basis upon which to choose, what else could one feel? He feels what many of us feel, having little more basis for our choices than he had for his.

This lack of basis along with the feelings that the lack produces helps explain the last stanza of Frost's poem. Here, the speaker takes us from the past (stanzas 1-3) to the distant future ("ages and ages hence"--13), suggesting thereby how for us the past remains present and always conditions the future. Sometime way in the future, he tells us, he will say that his reason for choosing the road that he did was that it was "the one less travelled by" (19), the one that "was grassy and wanted wear" (8). But we know that this will be a rationalization for a choice made regretfully and without any real basis. Yet who among us would say, "I chose my college, my career, my wife or husband by the flip of a coin"? Psychologically, we need to feel that we have chosen, even if--no, especially if--chance has been what in fact has directed us. And when enough time has gone by, we do start to remember reasons for choices that had no rational basis in fact. Frost's speaker underscores this process, which Fromm calls "the art of disremembering" (Loving 89), by his projection into the future of his future distortion of the past.

"The Road Not Taken," then, concerns the difficulty that choice entails for us: our reluctance to choose, our mixed feelings once we have chosen, and our tendency to rationalize our choices at some later date. We must choose, but making choices is difficult both because of the imponderables of the external world and especially--as Frost drives home--because of the conflicts within. The irony of it is that, unlike most people who have lived on this earth, we have the luxury of choice but often find that luxury burdensome. Freedom of choice, it seems, brings its own set of problems and its own psychological dilemmas.

Works Cited

Fromm, Eric. <u>The Art of Loving</u>. New York: Harper, 1956.

---. <u>Escape from Freedom</u>. New York: Harper, 1951.

Frost, Robert. "The Road Not Taken." <u>Responding to Literature</u>.
    Ed. Judith A. Stanford. Mountain View: Mayfield, 1992, 5.

Loewald, Hans. <u>Psychoanalysis and the History of the Individual </u>.
    New Haven: Yale UP, 1978.

Lynen, John. "Frost as Modern Poet." <u>Robert Frost: A Collection
    of Critical Essays</u>. Ed. James M. Cox. Englewood Cliffs:
    Prentice, 1962. 177-97.

Mill, John Stuart. "The Subjugation of Women." <u>Essays on Sexual
    Equality</u>. Ed. A. S. Rossi. Chicago: U of Chicago P, 1970.
    143-68.

Proffitt, Edward. "Frost's Journey from Gloom." <u>Research
    Studies</u> 44.4. (1976): 248-51.

Index

Achtert, Walter S., 177
Active voice, 128, 130
Adjectives, 143, 158–159
Adverbs, 42,158–159
After, 42
"Air, the Water, the Waste, The" (Ji-Hoon), 87–88
Allusion, 165
Although, 42
Analogy
  in beginnings, 30
  in endings, 67–68
  as method of paragraph development, 79, 82
Analytic prose, 3
  example of, 5–6
  thesis of, 17
And, 43, 157
Anecdotes, 31–32
Anthologies, 178–179
Appeal to authority, 79, 81–82
Argument, 66
Articles
  journal, 177–178
  newspaper, 179–180
Audience, 7–9
Authority, appeal to, 79, 81–82
Autobiographical essays, 100–102

Balanced syntax, 137
Because, 42
Beginnings, 29–36
  analogy in, 30
  anecdotes in, 31–32
  contrast in, 30–31
  from familiar to unfamiliar in, 33
  from general to particular in, 34
Bendernagle, Edward, 31, 67

Biographical essays, 100
Blocked comparison and contrast, 55–56
Blocked quotations, vs. continuous quotations, 169–170, 175
"Body and Soul" (Levins), 119–120
Books, citing, 177, 178, 180
Brainstorming, 22
"Bureaucrats" (Didion), 110
Burke, Mary Pat, 53
But, 43

Calvi, Sandra, 18–20, 21, 95–96, 100–102, 103–104, 115–116, 117, 175–176
Carifto, Judy, 82
Carroll, Jennifer, 108–109, 117
Categorization, 11
Cause and effect, 78, 80
Cazzola, Rae, 32
Character sketch, 108–109
Chronological sequence, 53, 85–84
Citations, 174–176
Classification method of paragraph development, 79
Climax, 69. *See also* Endings
  order of, 58–59, 87–88
Coherence, 48–52, 138–139
Comparison, 146, 159–160. *See also* Metaphorical language
Comparison and contrast
  as method of paragraph development, 79
  as pattern of organization, 54–56, 85–86
Complex sentences, 131
Compound-complex sentences, 131
Compound sentences, 131, 139
Conjunctions
  coordinating, 42–43
  subordinating, 42
Consequently, 42

Constructions, changing, 146–148
Continuous quotations, vs. blocked quotations, 169–170, 175
Contrast, 30–31. *See also* Comparison and contrast
Coordinating conjunctions, 42–43
"Court Day" (O'Connell), 123–125

Definition method of paragraph development, 79, 81
Degnan, Maureen, 28
de la Cruz, Joanne, 81
Description method of paragraph development, 79, 80
Details, fictional, 104
"Dialectical Spirituality" (McCarra), 89–90
Dialectical structure, 88–90
Dialogue, 103–104
Diction, 121–130
    formal, 121–122, 126, 127–130
    informal, 121, 122, 125–126
    ordinary, 121, 122, 126, 127–130
Didion, Joan, 110
Dinnell, Scott, 81
Discrete metaphor, 112, 113
Double negatives, 161
Draft
    first, 11–12
    second, 12–13. *See also* Revision

Ellipses, 171–172
Endings, 66–70
    analogy in, 67–68
    question and answer in, 68
    reverse funnel in, 68–69
    summarizing and restating in, 66–67
"Entertaining a Child" (Mulgrew), 99
Enumeration, 56–58, 86–87
Evaluation method of paragraph development, 79
Exemplification, 79, 80–81
Explicit metaphor, 111–112
Expository writing
    function of, 2
    goals of, 1–2
    types of, 2–7
Extended metaphor, 112, 113

Familiar, to unfamiliar, 33
Faulkner, William, 132
"Feud Burns On, The" (Mulgrew), 112
Fictional details, 104
Figurative language, 111–114
For, 43
For instance, 42
Formal style, 121–122, 126, 127–130

Forster, E. M., 1, 57–58, 106–107
Freewriting, 22
Frost, Robert, 4–7, 17–18, 22, 23, 24–25, 34, 50–52, 69, 71–76, 138–139, 170
Funnel paragraph, 29–36
    reverse, 68–69
    revision of, 34–36

Generalizations
    in beginnings, 34
    in endings, 69
"Gettysburg Address" (Lincoln), 135–137
Gibaldi, Joseph, 177
Gillin, Barry J., 58–59

Hemingway, Ernest, 131–132
Historical essays, 100
However, 42
Hoyt, Edward, 122–123

If, 42
Implicit metaphor, 111–112
Inference, logical, 79
Informal style, 121, 122, 125–126
Informational prose, 2
    example of, 5
    thesis of, 17
Italics, vs. quotation marks, 168–169

"Jaspers, The," 20, 21, 29, 39–43, 46, 48
Ji-Hoon, Ahn, 87–88
Journal articles, 177–178

Lalaina, Laura, 83–84, 90–94
"Late Night Thoughts on Listening to Mahler's Ninth Symphony" (Thomas), 114–115
Lau, Siu, 32, 67
"Lead-in," 29–36
Levins, P. J., 119–120
Lincoln, Abraham, 135–137
Logical inference, 79
Loose syntax, 132–133

Markey, Marge, 57
Masucci, Tracy, 44–45, 85–86, 117
Matesich, Arais, 33
"Matter of Face, A" (Masucci), 85–86, 117
McCarra, MaryAnn, 35–36, 89–90
McKeever, Ciaran, 84–85
McMahon, Claire, 31, 86–87, 114
"Memories of Me" (Lalaina), 83–84
Metaphorical language, 111–114
Middle (ordinary) style, 121, 122, 126, 127–130
Middles, 70–90

organizational patterns in, 71, 82–90
outlining, 76–77
paragraphing, 78–90
sample paper, 71–74
supports in, 75–76
topic sentences in, 70–71
Mixed metaphor, 113
MLA Handbook for Writers of Research Papers
    (Gibaldi and Achtert), 177
Modern Language Association of America,
    176–177
"Modest Proposal, A" (Swift), 105–106
Mulgrew, Terence, 31, 68, 99, 112
"My Best Friend" (Carroll), 108–109, 117
"My Dog" (Calvi), 18–20, 21, 175–176
"My Summer Job" (McMahon), 86–87, 114

Narration, 100–103
Nevertheless, 42
Newspaper articles, 179–180
Nor, 43, 164
Notes, 11
Noun phrases, 128, 130
Novak, Thomas, 82

O'Connell, William, 123–125
Official style, 127–130. *See also* Formal style
Opening paragraph, 29–36
Opinion, vs. thesis, 18
Or, 43, 157
Order of climax, 58–59, 87–88
Ordinary (middle) style, 121, 122, 126,
    127–130
Organization, 38–99
    of beginnings, 29–36
    coherence and, 48–52
    of endings, 66–70
    of first draft, 11–12
    of middles, 70–90
    of paragraphs, 12–13
    transitions and, 38–46, 71
    unity and, 46–52
"Organizational Cultures: A Contrast"
    (Lalaina), 90–94
Organizational patterns, 52–59, 71, 82–90
    chronology, 53, 83–84
    comparison and contrast, 54–56, 85–86
    dialectical structure, 88–90
    enumeration, 56–58, 86–87
    order of climax, 58–59, 87–88
    spatial sequence, 53–54, 84–85
Outlining, 76–77

Paragraph development, 78–82
    by analogy, 79, 82
    by appeal to authority, 79, 81–82

by definition, 79, 81
by exemplification, 79, 80–81
Paragraph(s)
    beginning, 29–36
    ending, 66–70
    middle, 78–90
    organization of, 12–13, 82–90
    thesis, 29–36
    topic sentence of, 70–71
    transitional, 43
Parallel syntax, 134–137
Paraphrasing, 168, 170, 173
Parenthetical citation, 174
Paring down, for sentence variety, 141–146
"Party Buddies" (Hoyt), 122–123
Passive voice, 128–129, 130
Patterns of organization. *See* Organizational
    patterns
Periodic syntax, 133
Persuasion, 1
Persuasive prose, 3
    example of, 6–7
    thesis of, 17
Phrases
    noun, 128, 130
    prepositional, 128, 130
    transitional, 38–39, 41–42
Plagiarism, 168
Poetic style, 122
Point-by-point comparison and contrast,
    54–55
Prepositional phrases, 128, 130
Prewriting, 10–11
Primary sources, 173–174
Proofreading, 13
Prosaic style, 122
Punctuation
    changing in quotations, 170–171
    ellipses, 171–172
    quotation marks, 168–170

Question and answer ending, 68
Quotation(s), 168–180
    changing punctuation in, 170–171
    citation of, 174–176
    continuous vs. blocked, 169–170, 175
    ellipses in, 171–172
    fitting with contexts, 172
    introducing, 172–173
    list of Works Cited, 176–180
    paraphrase vs., 173
    square brackets in, 171–172
    summary vs., 173
Quotation marks
    in continuous quotations, 169–170
    italics vs., 168–169

Quotation marks (*continued*)
  other punctuation with, 169–170
  single vs. double, 170–171

Reference, 165
Reiner, Alfred J., 54
Repetition, 43
Repositioning, for sentence variety,
  139–140
Restating, 66–67
Reversal, 30–31
Reverse funnel, 68–69
Revision
  of funnel paragraph, 34–36
  of good paper, 90–94
  transitions and, 39–43
  for unity and coherence, 47–52
Rewriting, 12–13
Rhetoric, 1–2
Rhyme, 114
Rhythm, 114–116, 140, 141
"Road Not Taken, The" (Frost), 4–7,
  17–18, 22, 23, 24–25, 34, 50–52, 69,
  71–76, 138–139, 170
"Rushing" (Degnan), 20

Secondary sources, 173–174
"Self-Expression" (McKeever), 84–85
Sentences
  length of, 138–139
  simplifying, 147–148
  topic, 70–71
  types of, 131–132
Sentence variety, 137–146
  paring down and, 141–146
  repositioning and, 139–140
  special effects and, 141
  substitution and, 140
Similes, 111
Simple sentences, 131, 138–139
So, 43, 165–166
"So Much for Philosophy!" (Calvi), 100–
  102, 103–104, 115–116, 117, 175–176
Sound, 114, 140
Sources, 168–180
  changing punctuation of, 170–171
  citing, 174–176
  in list of Works Cited, 176–180
  plagiarism and, 168
  primary, 173–174
  secondary, 173–174
  titles of, 168–169
  using, 168–173
Spatial sequence, 53–54, 84–85
Special effects, 141
Square brackets, 171–172

Statistics, 79, 80
Stroh, James, 30
Style, 121–153
  changing constructions, 146–148
  diction, 121–130
  formal, 121–122, 126, 127–130
  informal, 121, 122, 125–126
  official vs. ordinary, 127–130
  ordinary (middle), 121, 122, 126,
    127–130
  poetic, 122
  prosaic, 122
  sentence variety, 137–146
  syntax, 130–137
Subordinating conjunctions, 42
Substitution, for sentence variety, 140
Summaries
  in endings, 66–67
  of sources, 168, 170, 173
Supports
  major and minor, 75–76
  thesis and, 46–47
Swift, Jonathan, 105–106
Symbolism, 109–110
Syntax, 130–137
  balanced, 137
  loose, 132–133
  parallel, 134–137
  periodic, 133

Theme, 117
Therefore, 42
Thesis, 11, 17–37
  formulating, 21–23
  importance of, 18–21
  opinion vs., 18
  relationship with supporting material,
    46–47
  theme vs., 117
  topic vs., 17–18
  "useless" vs. useful knowledge and, 26–27
Thesis paragraph, 29–36
Thesis statement, 23–29
  following through on, 24–27
  location of, 27–29
Thomas, Lewis, 114–115
"Three Months with the Aboto" (Masucci),
  44–45
Thus, 42, 167
Titles, 13–14, 116–117
  of sources, 168–169
"Tolerance" (Forster), 105–106
Tone, 104–108
Topic, vs. thesis, 17–18
Topic sentence, 70–71
Transitional words and phrases, 38–39,

41–42
Transition(s), 38–46, 71
"Types of Men" (Calvi), 95–96

Unconscious, 12, 23
Unity, 46–52
Unless, 42
Usage, 155–167
" 'Useless' versus Useful Knowledge," 26–27

Variety. *See* Sentence variety
Verbiage, 128–130, 142–144. *See also* Formal style
Voice, 104–108
   passive vs. active, 128–130

When, 42
White, E. B., 143
Word(s), transitional, 38–39, 41–42
Wordiness, 128–130, 142–144. *See also* Formal style
Works Cited list, 174, 176–180
Writing process, 9–14
   prewriting, 10–11
   proofing and titling, 13–14
   rewriting, 12–13
   writing, 11–12

Yet, 43